The

Snapple™

Aptitude Test

SANDY WOOD & KARA KOVALCHIK

The Snapple™ Aptitude Test

By Sandy Wood
and Kara Kovalchik

A Stonesong Press Book
Broadway Books   New York

The Snapple™ Aptitude Test

Table of Contents

When we at Snapple say we put only the Best Stuff in our bottles, we don't just stop at the sipping part. There's a Real Fact printed under each and every one of our caps. Our Real Facts are almost as great as our drinks; you get to learn something new as you sip. Folks loved our Real Facts so much that we decided to go crazy and create our own SAT—*The Snapple Aptitude Test: Real Facts for Real Life.* And trust us, this is one test you'll enjoy taking!

Now, we all know there are a lot of products in this world that promise to make you a better person— smarter, more interesting, happier, and even better looking. But will *The Snapple Aptitude Test* do all those things? Actually, yes (well, except for the "better looking" part). This book *will* make you smarter. It's full of all kinds of quirky, amazing little facts about the world that will stretch your mind—1,000 questions in all! Don't worry; we don't expect anyone to score a perfect 1,000 on *The Snapple Aptitude Test*, although if you do, you can call yourself a Real Genius. Here are our scoring categories:

Real Genius	1,000 Points Total!
Fact Fanatic	900-999 Points
Seriously Cerebral	800-899 Points
Brainy	700-799 Points
Snapple Savant	600-699 Points
Egghead	500-599 Points
Sharpie	400-499 Points
Radio-FACT-tive	300-399 Points
Not Too Shabby	200-299 Points
Factose Intolerant	100-199 Points
Newbie	10-99 Points
Cro-Magnon	0-9 Points

Consider yourself warned: *The Snapple Aptitude Test* isn't your mother's trivia collection. While you will find plenty of multiple-choice questions, we've thrown in several twists to keep you on your toes. You'll find match-up questions, fill-in-the-blank questions, even some wordplay.

With the exception of you Real Geniuses out there, you're not going to know every answer to every question. Thus you will be learning something and therefore you'll become smarter!

The Snapple Aptitude Test will make you more interesting because you will now know things that other people don't, and you can talk about these interesting tidbits at school, parties, in job interviews, on dates, or even on line at the grocery store. Your vast knowledge of so many different subjects will draw others to you. After they have met you they will go home thinking, "Gee, that **[INSERT YOUR NAME HERE]** sure is interesting!"

Will *The Snapple Aptitude Test* make you a happier person? Of course! Now that you are filled with a library of super cool info and are surrounded by people who find you fascinating, you will indeed be happier.

What other book can make these kinds of assurances? It's bold, but, hey, we're Snapple and we're used to doing things like that.

Now sharpen those Number 2 pencils!

Ick-O-System

SCIENCE, NATURE &
THE HUMAN BODY

While some people are looking for signs of intelligent life in outer space, we're on the hunt for it right here on Earth! If you're one of the many who is blinded by science, the ICK-O-SYSTEM section of *The Snapple Aptitude Test* might open your eyes to this great universe and all the fascinating secrets it holds.

And best of all, you won't have to dissect a frog.

1. Which of the following containers would come closest to holding the amount of blood in a typical adult human's body?

    a. a one-quarter pitcher
    b. a two-liter bottle
    c. a one-gallon jug
    d. a two-gallon jug

2. Tasting something with the very tip of your tongue will tell you if it is:

    a. bitter
    b. sweet
    c. salty
    d. sour

3. True or False: Bulls are colorblind and cannot see the color red.

4. If the sun were a human of average lifespan, how old would it be?

    a. 5 years old
    b. a teenager
    c. in its 30s
    d. retirement age

5. Where did most of Skylab land when it crashed to Earth in 1979?

   a. Pacific Ocean
   b. Australia
   c. Siberia
   d. Antarctica

6. True or False: Russia's Sputnik I, the world's first satellite, was a tiny device less than two feet in diameter.

7. Nocturnal enuresis is the medical term for what sleeping disorder?

   a. bedwetting
   b. sleepwalking
   c. grinding your teeth
   d. talking in your sleep

8. No living species of bird has more than _____ toes.

   a. two
   b. three
   c. four
   d. five

9. The Magnetic North Pole is moving slowly away from _____ and toward _____.

   a. Greenland, Iceland
   b. Canada, Russia
   c. Norway, Sweden
   d. Alaska, Siberia

10. In the average American home, nearly 75 percent of incoming fresh water is used where?

    a. kitchen
    b. bathroom
    c. yard
    d. laundry room

11. Which of these creatures perennially causes the sudden deaths of more Americans than any other mammal (except humans)?

    a. wolves
    b. deer
    c. dogs
    d. horses

YOU COULDN'T PLANET ANY BETTER

Each planet in our Solar System will be the correct answer for one of the following nine questions. Place the correct planet names in the blanks.

12. Which ringed planet is closest to our sun?

    _____

13. Which planet is closest in size to Venus?

    _____

14. Which planet was discovered in the 18th century?

    _____

15. Which planet's orbit is on a markedly different plane than all others?

   _____

16. The surface of which planet gets the warmest?

   _____

17. Which planet has only two known moons?

   _____

18. Which was the farthest planet from the Sun from 1979-99?

   _____

19. Which planet's diameter is about 40 percent that of Earth's?

   _____

20. Which is the second-largest planet in the Solar System?

   _____

21. Wilhelm Roentgen used the letter X to reference X-Strahlen (what we now call X-rays) for what reason?

   a. his son, Xander
   b. their unknown source
   c. the rays physically cross
   d. the Roman numeral for 10

22. What's the *real* purpose of the large orange or red balls sometimes seen attached to high-tension power lines?

    a. to help hold up lines; they are filled with gas
    b. to absorb lightning strikes
    c. to help repair crews find them in the dark
    d. to provide visible warning for low-flying aircraft

23. How many muscles make up the trunk of an adult elephant?

    a. 3
    b. 18
    c. 290
    d. 40,000+

24. In 1959, the USSR's Mechta became the very first man-made satellite to orbit the Sun. What was the key reason that this seemingly amazing feat disappointed Soviet scientists?

25. Which automotive part shares its name with a word meaning "a group of eggs"?

    a. battery
    b. clutch
    c. muffler
    d. axle

26. The *tapetum lucidum* gives a cat the ability to:

    a. purr and meow
    b. see at night
    c. land on its feet
    d. wag its tail

27. What element is represented by the symbol A in the Periodic Table?

    a. arsenic
    b. argon
    c. aluminum
    d. none of the above

28. Which of the following could be found on the surface of the Earth?

    a. meteorite
    b. meteor
    c. meteoroid
    d. none of the above

29. Many common fruits, including apples, peaches, pears, and plums, are members of the same family as which of the following flowers?

    a. geraniums
    b. begonias
    c. asters
    d. roses

30. The "normal" human body temperature of 98.6° F. translates to approximately what number on the Celsius scale?

    a. 18
    b. 26
    c. 37
    d. 45

TEA TRUE?
Here are five True or False questions about
the most Snapple-y of drinks, tea!

31. Tea is a great beverage to drink with spicy foods, since the tannic acid in the tea helps to draw heat from the body.

32. Chamomile tea can be used to lighten a person's hair color.

33. Tea is fermented with a specific type of yeast that is native only to eastern Asia.

34. In Japan, a soup made of green tea and white rice is used as a common remedy for upset stomachs.

35. A 2005 study found that the combination of "milk and lemon" is the most common way Americans drink their hot tea.

36. Which planet interferes with the Solar System's symmetry of planets, which (based on increasing distance from the Sun) grow gradually larger and then smaller?

37. How many total natural teeth does a typical human being use in a lifetime?

38. What is the name of the muscle that contracts to bend the arm at the elbow?

39. This flightless bird can outrun a racehorse.

    a. kiwi
    b. penguin
    c. emu
    d. ostrich

40. Cats and dogs are owned by more U.S. households than any other pets. What's next on the list?

    a. hamsters
    b. fish
    c. canaries
    d. parakeets

41. In 1911, Casimir Funk identified (and coined the name of) which of the following?

    a. steroids
    b. vitamins
    c. amino acids
    d. carbohydrates

42. In the Pythagorean Theorem, $A^2 + B^2 = C^2$, the "C" is always:

    a. the longest side
    b. the side opposite the right angle
    c. both a and b
    d. neither a nor b

43. Yes or No: Should you be worried if your doctor has to perform an auscultation?

44. Mars' two moons, Deimos and Phobos, were named after the Roman god of war's _____.

    a. brothers
    b. parents
    c. horses
    d. swords

45. _____ percent of Americans donate blood each year.

46. True or False: Lettuce originally contained a narcotic liquid in its center, a trait bred out over many decades.

47. In today's world, what animals are most commonly used to hunt truffles?

    a. pigs
    b. squirrels
    c. moles
    d. dogs

48. Which theory did Albert Einstein devise first: the General Theory of Relativity or the Special Theory of Relativity?

49. Which has more bones, the human arm or the human leg?

50. Who coined the phrase "survival of the fittest"?

VOWEL OBSTRUCTION

Each of the three answers below contains five missing consonants. Place them in the blanks in the correct order and the answer to each clue will appear.

51. Plant family that includes belladonna.

    N I _ _ _ _ _ A D E

52. Uranium ore first studied by Pierre and Marie Curie in the late 19th century.

    P I _ _ _ _ _ E N D E

53. The equivalent of 1/100,000,000ths of a centimeter.

    A _ _ _ _ _ O M

54. The first full-organ transplant occurred in 1954 and involved a kidney removed from a _____ and placed into _____.

    a. father, his son
    b. brother, his twin
    c. baboon, its infant
    d. woman, her sister

Use the terms **DUODENUM**, **GALLBLADDER**, and **LIVER** to correctly fill in the blanks in the following sentence: Bile is produced by the ___#55___ stored in the ___#56___ and released into the ___#57___.

55. _____

56. _____

57. _____

58. What blood type makes a person a *universal recipient* (meaning he or she can accept blood of any other type)?

    a. Type A
    b. Type B
    c. Type AB
    d. Type O

59. Herpes can cause which of the following ailments?

    a. chickenpox
    b. shingles
    c. cold sores
    d. all of the above

60. True or False: Before aspirin was first produced, ill patients chewed the bark of the white willow tree to help alleviate fever and pain.

ICK-O-SYSTEM: SCIENCE, NATURE & THE HUMAN BODY

61. Beta-blocking drugs directly affect which part of the body?

    a. heart
    b. stomach
    c. brain
    d. bones

62. True or False: Despite its name, *Salmonella* may be found in most types of meat, but *not* in seafood.

63. True or False: In addition to his work in atomic theory and physics, Albert Einstein helped patent several refrigerator designs.

64. The key goal of alchemists, which was never achieved, was the ability to turn _____ into _____.

    a. other metals / gold
    b. water / blood
    c. hydrogen / oxygen
    d. bases / acids

65. Given the following three facts:
    • Halley's Comet last approached Earth in 1986.
    • Halley's Comet returns to Earth every 76 years.
    • Halley's Comet has been seen three times since Halley made his first prediction.

    Calculate the year that Edmund Halley first predicted the comet bearing his name would return to Earth.

66. A horizontal line over the top of a Roman numeral indicates that its value is:

    a. a negative number
    b. multiplied by 1,000
    c. used in a fraction
    d. none of the above

67. Which of the following parts of the head does not contain any taste buds?

    a. the uvula
    b. the tongue
    c. the roof of the mouth
    d. the throat

68. True or False: The *Australopithecus afarensis* hominid skeleton found in Ethiopia in 1974 was nicknamed Lucy in honor of the Beatles' song, "Lucy in the Sky with Diamonds."

69. Which of the following is true about Apollo XI astronaut Buzz Aldrin?

    a. his legal name is Buzz
    b. MTV's video music awards are named for him
    c. his mother's maiden name was Moon
    d. all of the above

70. What's the only month of the year that can end without seeing at least one full moon?

JUST ADD SNAPPLE!

To answer the following question, place the seven letters that make up "SNAPPLE" in the correct blanks:

71. What medical condition causes people to breathe slowly (or even stop breathing) when asleep?

    _ _ E _ _   A _ _ E _

72. Celebrities longing for a better defined *philtrum* and a more pronounced *cupid's bow* often receive collagen injections in what body part?

73. When he wasn't busy as emperor of Japan, Hirohito enjoyed spending his time in pursuit of what field of scientific research?

    a. marine biology
    b. reproductive theory
    c. astronomy
    d. botany

AN "A" FOR EFFORT

In this quiz, the word(s) in each answer are special in that they contain no vowels *other than* A. You won't find an E, an I, an O, or a U in any of them. We even took out Y, just in case.

74. This can be triggered by pollutants, smoke, allergies, or even cold air: _____

75. *Filé* is a Cajun food additive made of the powdered leaves of what plant? _____

76. This fastest species of snake can move at an incredible speed of 20 mph: _____

77. He's the man we have to thank for quantum theory: _____

78. Researchers believe that many UFO and ghost sightings are a result of the methane in:

_____

79. In total, how many Apollo astronauts set foot on the Moon?

80. Which of the following gives the Sacagawea dollar coin its distinctive color?

    a. nickel
    b. gold
    c. brass
    d. bronze

81. True or False: No bears are native to the continent of Australia.

82. The Rock of Gibraltar, located on the United Kingdom's colony of Gibraltar off the tip of Spain, is made of what type of stone?

83. Which mathematical formula calculates the circumference of a circle?

    a. 2πr
    b. πd
    c. both A and B
    d. neither A nor B

84. True or False: In lieu of cucumber slices, fans of natural remedies actually place cold, wet tea bags on their eyes to reduce puffiness.

85. True or False: The "funny bone" and the humerus (pronounced "humorous") are located in the same part of the body: the arm.

UP, UP, AND AWAY

This quiz is for the birds.

86. Studies in zero-gravity chambers have concluded that birds could not survive in weightlessness because they would not be able to:

   a. balance themselves
   b. ingest food
   c. lay eggs
   d. fight infections

87. True or False: Uncooked rice is dangerous to many birds, as their digestive juices cause it to expand inside the body, potentially causing internal injuries.

88. What type of birds did prisoner Robert Stroud keep and study while imprisoned at Alcatraz?

   a. canaries
   b. pigeons
   c. robins
   d. none of the above

89. *Abbott's, blue-footed, red-footed, brown,* and *masked* are all types of what genus of seabird?

90. True or False: Only one of the 17 types of penguin lives in areas north of the Equator.

91. In cartoons, what creature *(Canis latrans)* was given "alternate" scientific names, like *Eatius birdius* and *Hard-headed ravenus*?

    a. chickenhawk
    b. panther
    c. coyote
    d. none of the above

92. Bachelor's buttons, Lady's slippers, Bishop's hats, and Granny's bonnets aren't clothing items, but rather_____

93. Which of the following is stored inside a camel's hump?

    a. water
    b. air
    c. fat
    d. undigested food

94. Which of these pro sports teams is not named after a bird of prey?

    a. Atlanta Hawks
    b. Toronto Raptors
    c. Baltimore Ravens
    d. Atlanta Falcons

95. True or False: Green potato chips contain poison that can, eaten in enough quantity, affect the human body.

VENOM US

Following are five creatures that you don't want to stumble upon (particularly when they're in a fighting mood). Each of them can inject venom into their enemies. Identify the method used by each creature.

96. Brown recluse spider
    a. fangs
    b. stingers
    c. spurs
    d. spines

97. Jellyfish
    a. fangs
    b. stingers
    c. spurs
    d. spines

98. Lionfish
    a. fangs
    b. stingers
    c. spurs
    d. spines

99. Platypus
    a. fangs
    b. stingers
    c. spurs
    d. spines

100. Scorpion
    a. fangs
    b. stingers
    c. spurs
    d. spines

1. C

2. B

3. TRUE
It's the motion of the cape that causes bulls to charge.

4. C
The sun is a little less than halfway through its 10 billion year life span.

5. B

6. TRUE
Sputnik was a sphere measuring about 23 inches in diameter and weighing approximately 185 lbs.

7. A

8. C

9. B
The magnetic poles have long been known to move around. Scientists believe this is due to several factors, including slight changes in the rotation of the Earth's outer core.

10. B
The average American household uses approximately 185 gallons of water a day.

11. B
Human beings are the mammals that kill the most humans in the U.S. Second on the list are deer, which kill around 175 people annually in automobile accidents.

12. JUPITER
Jupiter has faint rings, as do Neptune and Uranus.

13. EARTH

14. URANUS

15. PLUTO

16. VENUS
While not the closest to the Sun, Venus's thick atmosphere makes it the warmest planet.

17. MARS

18. NEPTUNE
Pluto's distance from the Sun varies. Most of the time, it is the farthest planet from the Sun, but from 1979 to 1999 Pluto was closer to the Sun than Neptune.

19. MERCURY

20. SATURN

21. B
The first person to use X to indicate an unknown was René Descartes.

22. D

23. D

24. IT HAD BEEN AIMED AT THE MOON
(but missed by 5,000 miles)

25. B

26. B
The *tapetum lucidum* is a layer of light-reflecting cells behind a cat's eye. It is what gives them that odd glowing effect when a light is shined at them.

27. D

No element uses the symbol A. Aluminum is Al, argon is Ar, and arsenic is As.

28. A

A meteoroid is the object in space. In Earth's atmosphere, it's called a meteor. A meteorite is what's left when it reaches the Earth's surface.

29. D

They're all members of the same order as roses.

30. C

31. TRUE

32. TRUE

33. FALSE

Tea isn't fermented with yeast at all. It's actually the cutting and bruising of the leaves that cause them to turn dark.

34. TRUE

35. FALSE

If you've ever made the mistake of doctoring your tea this way, you know that the lemon juice curdles the milk into an icky mess. Most Americans drink their hot tea with sugar or honey.

36. MARS

Moving away from the sun, each planet grows progressively larger until Jupiter, after which they grow progressively smaller. Only Mars (which perhaps was, at one time, larger than the Earth) interrupts this pattern.

37. 52

20 baby teeth + 32 permanent teeth.

38. BICEPS

39. D

40. D

41. B

42. C

43. NO

It's simply the process of listening to some part of your body through a stethoscope.

44. C

The horses pulled Mars's war chariot.

45. FIVE

About 60 percent of the American population is eligible to donate blood.

46. TRUE

47. D

Truffles contain a steroid that excites female pigs. Dogs proved just as able at locating them, however, and are easier to maintain.

48. SPECIAL THEORY

Einstein's Special Theory of Relativity, better known as $E=mc^2$, appeared in 1905; the General Theory was announced 11 years later.

49. ARM

Each of our arms has 32 bones; each of our legs has only 31.

50. HERBERT SPENCER

This 19th-century British philosopher and scientist came up with the phrase as a way to describe Darwin's theory of natural selection.

51. (NI)GHTSH(ADE)

52. (PI)TCHBL(ENDE)

53. (A)NGSTR(OM)

54. B

The donor's twin brother survived for seven years with the new kidney.

55. LIVER

56. GALLBLADDER

57. DUODENUM

58. C

59. D

60. TRUE

For centuries, the white willow tree was used for medicinal purposes, including pain relief.

61. C

Beta-blockers block impulses in the brain, indirectly reducing the rate and force of contractions in the heart.

62. FALSE

63. TRUE

64. A

65. 1758

The comet did appear that year, as well as in 1834 and 1910. It is expected to return in 2062.

66. B

Numbers over 1,000 aren't represented with their own Roman numeral characters, so a line is drawn over a V (5) to represent 5,000 or an X (10) to represent 10,000 (and so on).

67. A

68. TRUE

69. D

70. FEBRUARY

The time from full moon to full moon is about 29.5 days, so only a month with fewer than 29.5 days could ever miss having at least one full moon. This only occurs about four times a century.

71. SLEEP APNEA

72. THE LIPS

73. A

74. AN ASTHMA ATTACK

75. SASSAFRAS

76. BLACK MAMBA

77. MAX KARL PLANCK

78. MARSH or SWAMP GAS

79. 12
Armstrong, Aldrin, Bean, Cernan, Conrad, Duke, Irwin, Mitchell, Schmitt, Scott, Shepard, and Young.

80. C
The copper/zinc alloy gave the coin its gold tone.

81. TRUE
Koala bears aren't bears.

82. LIMESTONE

83. C
Since the radius of a circle is half the diameter, the two formulae have the same value.

84. TRUE

85. TRUE
Some suggest that the "funny bone" got its name as a pun on the bone's name, but the "funny bone" is really not a bone at all; it's a spot on the *ulnar nerve*.

86. B
Birds require gravity in order to swallow. Without it, they cannot eat.

87. FALSE
An urban legend that this occurs after rice is thrown at weddings has been circulating for many years, but it has been proven untrue.

88. D
The murderer's bird studies—specifically canaries—were done at Leavenworth Prison. Despite his nickname, the Birdman of Alcatraz, he was not allowed to keep birds at that prison.

89. BOOBIES
They were so-named by sailors, who felt the birds were stupid since they were easy to catch.

90. TRUE
The Galapagos Penguin may be found north of the equator on Isabela Island.

91. C

92. PLANTS

93. C
A camel can live off this fat if left without food, and the hump will decrease in size as the camel's body uses the fat for energy.

94. C

95. TRUE
Green potato chips contain a toxic alkaloid called solanine. You'd have to eat about five pounds of these chips before feeling sick (but five pounds of regular chips would make anyone sick!).

96. A

97. B

98. D

99. C

100. B

2

War & Peace
History & World Leaders

Attention hawks and doves! Get ready to play war games on the world's battlefields or negotiate at its peace parleys. Here you can take up arms and see if you make the same guesses as the kings, dictators, presidents, premiers, and other statesmen did in their times. With apologies to George Santayana: Those who cannot learn from the WAR AND PEACE section of *The Snapple Aptitude Test* are doomed to repeat it.

1. Before the outbreak of the American Revolution, which of the following harbor towns was involved in an attack upon tea-bearing ships?

   a. Annapolis, Maryland
   b. Boston, Massachusetts
   c. Charleston, South Carolina
   d. all of the above

2. In Britain and Europe, the first Battles Royale involved what type of fights?

   a. boxing matches
   b. pistol duels
   c. cockfights
   d. fencing matches

3. Plato's first Academy, opened in 387 B.C. and widely considered to be the first school of higher learning in the Western world, was located in:

   a. an olive grove
   b. a church
   c. a cave
   d. a mausoleum

4. Which side was defeated at the Battle of the Alamo in 1836?

   a. Mexico
   b. United States
   c. Spain
   d. none of the above

5. What state put the U.S. Constitution into effect when it became the ninth state to ratify the document (providing a majority)?

   a. North Carolina
   b. Maryland
   c. New Hampshire
   d. New Jersey

TAKING A "NAP"

Match the island choices in column B with the appropriate blanks in column A.

Napoleon Bonaparte was born in ____#6____, was exiled to ____#7____, and died in ____#8____.

COLUMN A	COLUMN B
6. _____	Elba
7. _____	St. Helena
8. _____	Corsica

AN "A" FOR EFFORT

In this quiz, the word(s) in each answer are special in that they contain no vowels *other than* A. You won't find an E, an I, an O, or a U in any of them. We even took out Y, just in case.

9. Virginia site of the Battles of Bull Run during the U.S. Civil War: _____

10. Later assassinated, he shared the 1978 Nobel Peace Prize: _____

11. In 1912–13, these conflicts led to the breakup of the Ottoman Empire: _____

12. Colloquial name of the flag used by the Confederate States of America: _____

13. The post–WWII European Recovery Program was commonly referred to as the: _____

COMMANDERS-IN-CHIEF

14. Besides Franklin Delano Roosevelt, what other man won the popular vote in three consecutive presidential elections?

15. Teddy Roosevelt was the first U.S. president to:

    a. ride in a car
    b. submerge in a submarine
    c. fly in an airplane
    d. all of the above

16. Who was U.S. president in 1841?

    a. John Tyler
    b. William Henry Harrison
    c. Martin Van Buren
    d. all of the above

17. Fill in the blanks: _____ was president of the United States in the _____.

    a. Warren G. Harding, 1920s
    b. Teddy Roosevelt, 1890s
    c. John Adams, 1910s
    d. Dwight D. Eisenhower, 1940s

18. Which 20th century U.S. president shared the same first name as his vice-president?

19. When submitted in September 1789, how many amendments originally made up the Bill of Rights (though only 10 of them were ratified)?

20. Edmund Ironside, Harold Harefoot, and Edward Longshanks were:

    a. kings of England
    b. early political cartoon characters
    c. colonial sailing ships
    d. Native American chiefs

21. Which of these "Great" monarchs ruled Russia?

    a. Ivan the Great
    b. Peter the Great
    c. Catherine the Great
    d. all of the above

22. Which U.S. president requested the return of Harry S. Truman's "The Buck Stops Here" sign to the White House?

    a. Ronald Reagan
    b. Richard Nixon
    c. Jimmy Carter
    d. George W. Bush

23. In July 2005, a U.S. postage stamp featured an image of _____ and _____ having tea together.

    a. Winston Churchill, Franklin D. Roosevelt
    b. Alice, the Mad Hatter
    c. Meriwether Lewis, William Clark
    d. Louisa May Alcott, Mark Twain

AMERICAN HISTORY

24. What U.S. state was named for Thomas West?

25. What U.S. state's capitol building is a smaller-scale replica of the one in Washington, D.C.?

    a. California
    b. Arkansas
    c. Michigan
    d. Florida

26. How many men and women were burned at the stake following their convictions at the Salem Witch Trials in the late 17ᵗʰ century?

27. Which Amendment to the U.S. Constitution abolished slavery in 1865?

    a. 19th Amendment
    b. 10th Amendment
    c. 13th Amendment
    d. 16th Amendment

(NATION)-LEADING LADIES
Who was the first female prime minister of:

28. ... Canada? _____

29. ... the United Kingdom? _____

30. ... India? _____

31. ... Israel? _____

32. ... Pakistan? _____

Identify the proper series of names:

33. _____ died the same year that _____ was born.

    a. George Washington, Abraham Lincoln
    b. Michelangelo, Shakespeare
    c. Marilyn Monroe, Madonna
    d. none of the above

34. True or False: Bricks made of dried tea were once used by Asian merchants as currency.

35. What U.S. land purchase involved the largest amount of land area?

    a. Alaska Purchase
    b. Louisiana Purchase
    c. Mexican Cession
    d. Gadsden Purchase

36. What were the only two U.S. states admitted to the Union on the very same date?

37. The first state to join the U.S. in the 19th century begins with the same letter as the first state to join in the 20th century. They were:

    a. Wisconsin and Wyoming
    b. Ohio and Oklahoma
    c. Maine and Montana
    d. Illinois and Idaho

38. Which of these presidents, all of whom died in office, doesn't belong with the others?

    a. Warren G. Harding
    b. Franklin D. Roosevelt
    c. Zachary Taylor
    d. William McKinley

39. The first civilization in the Western Hemisphere, the Olmecs, worshiped what creature as their god?

    a. wolf
    b. jaguar
    c. buffalo
    d. dragon

40. Who was the only "third party" presidential candidate to grab more than 25 percent of the popular vote?

    a. Eugene V. Debs
    b. Theodore Roosevelt
    c. George Wallace
    d. H. Ross Perot

41. What 100-story Chicago structure was completed in 1969?

LODGING COMPLAINTS

Following are the names of five well-known persons and five rather infamous places to stay. Place the two correct entries in each set of blanks below.

PEOPLE

DIANA, PRINCESS OF WALES
ROBERT KENNEDY
DR. MARTIN LUTHER KING, JR.
BENJAMIN "BUGSY" SIEGEL
FRANK WILLS

PLACES

AMBASSADOR HOTEL
FLAMINGO HOTEL
LORRAINE MOTEL
RITZ HOTEL
WATERGATE HOTEL

42. In Washington, D.C., in 1972, _____ noticed a break-in at the _____ , which led to a national political scandal.

43. The _____ in Memphis, Tennessee, now home to a museum, was the site of the assassination of _____.

44. A year before he was gunned down by mobsters, _____ opened the first hotel on the Las Vegas Strip, the _____.

45. Sirhan Sirhan had a fatal encounter with _____ at the _____ in Los Angeles.

46. Security cameras at the _____ in Paris recorded some of the last photos of _____.

47. This was the world's largest passenger ship in 1915 when it sank, claiming more than a thousand victims. Name it.

48. True or False: Foreign workers with the highest level of diplomatic immunity may not be given a traffic ticket.

49. How old was the Berlin Wall when it came tumbling down, reuniting the city?

    a. 104 years
    b. 61 years
    c. 51 years
    d. 28 years

50. Abigail Smith Adams was:

    a. John Adams' wife
    b. John Quincy Adams' grandmother
    c. both A and B
    d. neither A nor B

51. Which of these former U.S. presidents passed away just a few months before Apollo 11 landed on the moon in 1969?

    a. Harry Truman
    b. Lyndon B. Johnson
    c. Dwight D. Eisenhower
    d. Herbert Hoover

S.A. ESSAY

Below is the world's shortest essay about South Africa (or at least the shortest one we've ever written). It's missing three names, and you'll fill them in by using three of the four names in the following list (one name on this list will *not* be used).

LIST OF NAMES:

| P.W. BOTHA | F.W. DE KLERK |
| NELSON MANDELA | DESMOND TUTU |

In 1989, ___#52___ resigned as president of South Africa and was succeeded by ___#53___. who shared the 1993 Nobel Peace Prize with ___#54___.

52. _____

53. _____

54. _____

55. Which future president was U.S. ambassador to the United Nations from 1971 to 1973?

a. Gerald Ford
b. Jimmy Carter
c. Ronald Reagan
d. George H. W. Bush

56. Over the last 50 years, only one third-party presidential candidate has garnered any electoral votes. Name him.

a. H. Ross Perot
b. John B. Anderson
c. John G. Schmitz
d. George C. Wallace

57. How many children were fathered by George Washington, known as the Father of Our Country?

58. What city's Board of Education was involved in the famous 1954 Supreme Court decision known as *Brown v. Board of Education*?

Name the two future U.S. presidents who signed:

59. the Declaration of Independence

_____ and _____

60. the U.S. Constitution

_____ and _____

VOWEL OBSTRUCTION

Each of the three answers below contains five missing consonants. Place them in the blanks in the correct order and the answer to each clue will appear.

61. Confederate general said to have caused the rebel defeat at Gettysburg.

    L O _ _ _ _ _ E E T

62. A torture device that was painful, though not fatal.

    T H U _ _ _ _ _ E W

63. Last name of a German family who hit it big in banking.

    R O _ _ _ _ _ I L D

64. Nicholas Breakspear was the name of the first Englishman to become:

    a. Poet Laureate
    b. Prime Minister
    c. Pope
    d. Prince of Wales

65. True or False: Judges began wearing black robes in 17th-century Britain to mourn the deaths of Charles II and Mary II, after which they became customary.

66. True or False: Made law in 2001, the PATRIOT Act is an acronym for "Providing Appropriate Tools Required to Intercept and Obstruct Terrorism."

67. What was the name of the first European settlement built in what is now the United States?

    a. San Miguel de Guadalupe
    b. Plymouth Rock
    c. Jamestown
    d. St. Augustine

68. In what city was the Liberty Bell, which became a key symbol of American independence, cast?

    a. Philadelphia
    b. Washington
    c. Rome
    d. London

PARDON ME

Most U.S. presidents haven't been shy to use their power to pardon. Four of the more well-known pardons occurred in the 1970s–80s, so in Column A, you'll see the name of four presidents from that era. Match them with the correct entries in Column B, a list of people who received a pardon.

COLUMN A	COLUMN B
69. RICHARD NIXON	A) PATRICIA HEARST
70. GERALD FORD	B) JIMMY HOFFA
71. JIMMY CARTER	C) TOKYO ROSE
72. RONALD REAGAN	D) GEORGE STEINBRENNER

73. True or False: Explorer Christopher Columbus sighted the South American mainland on one of his voyages to the Americas.

74. What came to Australia for the first time in late November of 1956?

    a. the Summer Olympics
    b. the World's Fair
    c. the president of the U.S.
    d. electricity

75. On March 28, 1979, which of the following islands made headline news?

    a. Falkland Islands (armed invasion)
    b. Hawaii (powerful earthquake)
    c. Manhattan (major blackout)
    d. Three Mile Island (nuclear accident)

76. President Gerald Ford encouraged Americans to wear buttons that said "WIN," an acronym that stood for _____.

77. What Spanish dictator's slow, lingering death in 1975 managed to become a long-running joke on TV's *Saturday Night Live*?

A ROYAL PAIN?

Here's the short version of the British royal family tree, including the Queen, her husband, and her four children.

PRINCE PHILIP #78 = HER MAJESTY QUEEN ELIZABETH II

PRINCE CHARLES #79 | PRINCESS ANNE (PRINCESS ROYAL) | PRINCE ANDREW #80 | PRINCE EDWARD #81

Anne's title (Princess Royal) already appears. Using the entries from the list of titles below, fill in these blanks as they match the men in Queen Elizabeth's life:

LIST OF TITLES

· DUKE OF EDINBURGH	· DUKE OF YORK
· EARL OF WESSEX	· PRINCE OF WALES

78. _____

79. _____

80. _____

81. _____

RULING EPITHETS

Royal types are all about names and titles, but sometimes history has given them some rather unusual descriptions. In each of the following sets, choose the one who was *not* a real ruler.

82. Who was not a ruler of France?

    a. Charles II (the Fat)
    b. Louis II (the Stammerer)
    c. John IV (the Weasel)
    d. Philip V (the Tall)

83. Who was not a ruler of England?

    a. Herman III (the Short)
    b. Ethelred II (the Unready)
    c. Alfred I (the Great)
    d. Canute I (the Dane)

84. Who was not a ruler of Germany?

    a. Henry III (the Black)
    b. Louis I (the Child)
    c. Stanley II (the Blind)
    d. Otto I (the Great)

PRINCESS PHONEYS

See how much you know about modern-day princesses. There is a lot more to them than just tiaras and toads.

85. True or False: In 2003, Princess Stephanie of Monaco, having failed in two marriages, got married a third time: to a circus acrobat.

86. True or False: Spain's Princess Letizia has announced that when she becomes queen, she will move the capital from Madrid to the coastal city of Barcelona.

87. True or False: Princess Masako of Japan was hospitalized for depression in 2003 after she failed to deliver the required male heir.

88. Joseph Hazelwood was the captain of what ill-fated vessel?

    a. *Edmund Fitzgerald*
    b. *Titanic*
    c. *Exxon Valdez*
    d. *Achille Lauro*

89. What U.S. Army officer was court-martialed as a result of his actions in My Lai, Vietnam?

    a. Eddie Slovik
    b. William Calley
    c. Barry Sadler
    d. Delmar Simpson

90. In 1981, President Ronald Reagan fired more than 11,000 striking members of PATCO, the union representing what profession?

JESSIES, GIRL!

Here we describe five females named Jessica, each of whom had her own footnote in history. From the list of last names, place the correct ones in the blanks provided.

DUBROFF   HAHN   LYNCH   McCLURE   SAVITCH

91. The first POW successfully recovered from Operation Iraqi Freedom: JESSICA _____.

92. Attempted to pilot a plane cross-country at the age of seven: JESSICA _____.

93. Controversial news anchor who spaced out while hosting an *NBC News Update* in 1983: JESSICA _____.

94. Secretary and mistress of former PTL leader Jim Bakker: JESSICA _____.

95. Was rescued after being trapped in a Texas well for 58 long hours: JESSICA _____.

FIVE-QUESTION ABs

Each question in this quiz begins with AB. No particular reason—those are just the first two letters that came to mind.

96. *AB*ZUG was the last name of the first member of the U.S. Congress to:

   a. represent the state of Hawaii
   b. be impeached from office
   c. have been born a Jewish woman
   d. be censured by the Senate

97. *AB*SCAM was the name of a discreet government operation initiated by the:

   a. FBI
   b. Department of Defense
   c. IRS
   d. DEA

98. *AB*OLITION was the political goal behind John Brown's 1859 attack on:

   a. Fort Sumter
   b. Bull Run
   c. Robert E. Lee
   d. Harper's Ferry

99. *AB*DICATION was a step taken by this House of Windsor monarch:

   a. Edward VIII
   b. George V
   c. George VII
   d. Elizabeth II

100. *AB*YSSINIA is the former name of what African nation, overrun by Italy in 1935?

   a. Sudan
   b. Ethiopia
   c. Mali
   d. Angola

1. **D**
   The Boston Tea Party was not the only confrontation, but it was certainly the most famous.

2. **C**
   They were cockfights in which more than two roosters took part.

3. **A**

4. **D**
   The Battle of the Alamo was fought between Mexico and the soon-to-be Republic of Texas. Mexico won the battle. Even when the fort was later re-taken from Mexico, Texas was denied admission into the U.S. for nearly a decade and chose to form its own nation (the Republic of Texas) instead.

5. **C**

6. **CORSICA**

7. **ELBA**

8. **ST. HELENA**

9. **MANASSAS**

10. **ANWAR AL-SADAT**

11. **BALKAN WARS**

12. **STARS AND BARS**
    The CSA flag had 13 stars, even though only 11 states were members of the Confederacy. Delaware and Kentucky were "unofficially" represented.

13. **MARSHALL PLAN**

14. **GROVER CLEVELAND**
    In his first re-election bid, while he won the popular vote, he lost the electoral vote to Benjamin Harrison.

15. **D**
    He was also the first sitting president to visit a foreign country when he traveled to Panama in 1906.

16. **D**
    Van Buren's term ended in March, when Harrison was inaugurated. He passed away in April, making Tyler the new president.

17. **A**
    Warren G. Harding defeated Democrat James Cox in the 1920 presidential election.

18. **WOODROW WILSON**
    Thomas Woodrow Wilson's vice president was Thomas R. Marshall.

19. **12**
    Two years after their first submission, the required number of states ratified 10 of the 12 amendments. The two amendments that were not ratified concerned the number of constituents for each Representative and the compensation for members of Congress.

20. **A**
    These three men ruled England in the 11th, 11th, and 14th-15th centuries, respectively.

21. **D**

22. **C**
    The sign had been at the Truman Library since 1957, before Carter's request was granted by Harry's daughter, Margaret. It was later returned to the Library.

23. **B**

24. **DELAWARE**
    West was a British colonial governor whose title was Baron de la Warr.

25. **B**

26. **NONE**
    Of the 20 that were executed, one was "pressed" to death while the other 19 were hanged.

27. **C**

28. **KIM CAMPBELL**

29. **MARGARET THATCHER**

30. **INDIRA GANDHI**

31. **GOLDA MEIR**

32. **BENAZIR BHUTTO**

33. **B**
The year in question was 1564.

34. **TRUE**

35. **B**

36. **NORTH** and **SOUTH DAKOTA**
Both joined on November 2, 1889. North Dakota was classified as the 39th state, South Dakota as the 40th.

37. **B**
Ohio joined the U.S. on March 1, 1803. Oklahoma became the 46th state on November 16, 1907.

38. **D**
All the others died of natural causes, while McKinley was assassinated.

39. **B**

40. **B**
Teddy pulled in 27 percent of the votes as the representative of his Bull Moose party in 1912.

41. **THE JOHN HANCOCK CENTER**
The Sears Tower, completed in 1974, is 10 stories taller.

42. **FRANK WILLS / WATERGATE HOTEL**

43. **LORRAINE MOTEL / DR. MARTIN LUTHER KING, JR.**

44. **BENJAMIN "BUGSY" SIEGEL / FLAMINGO HOTEL**

45. **ROBERT KENNEDY / AMBASSADOR HOTEL**

46. **RITZ HOTEL / DIANA, PRINCESS OF WALES**

47. **THE LUSITANIA**
The Titanic sank in 1912.

48. **FALSE**
While a high degree of diplomatic immunity protects from most types of prosecution, traffic citations may still be given.

49. **D**
The Berlin Wall was raised in 1961 and razed in 1989.

50. **A**
She was John Quincy Adams' mother, not grandmother.

51. **C**
Dwight D. Eisenhower died on March 28, 1969, and Herbert Hoover died October 20, 1964. At the time of the moon landing, Truman and LBJ were the only living ex-presidents.

52. **P.W. BOTHA**

53. **F.W. DE KLERK**

54. **NELSON MANDELA**

55. **D**

56. **D**

57. **NONE**
When George married widow Martha Dandridge Custis, he adopted her two children, but the couple never had any of their own.

58. **TOPEKA, KANSAS**

59. **JOHN ADAMS** and **THOMAS JEFFERSON**

60. **GEORGE WASHINGTON** and **JAMES MADISON**

61. (LO)NGSTR(EET)

62. (THU)MBSCR(EW)

63. (RO)THSCH(ILD)

64. **C**
    He became Pope Adrian IV in 1154.

65. **TRUE**

66. **TRUE**

67. **A**
    A group of Spaniards settled there in 1526, only to leave six months later. The spot is on the Atlantic coast near the border of Georgia and South Carolina.

68. **D**
    London's Whitechapel Foundry is known for two famous bells: the Liberty Bell and Big Ben.

69. **B**

70. **C**

71. **A**

72. **D**

73. **TRUE**
    On his third journey westward in 1498, he first visited the islands of Trinidad and Tobago and then sighted what is now the Venezuelan coast.

74. **A**
    Since they were held in the Southern Hemisphere, the games occurred much later in the year than normal so that the weather would be appropriately warm.

75. **D**

76. "WHIP INFLATION NOW"

77. **GENERALISSIMO FRANCISCO FRANCO**

78. **DUKE OF EDINBURGH**

79. **PRINCE OF WALES**

80. **DUKE OF YORK**

81. **EARL OF WESSEX**

82. **C**

83. **A**

84. **C**

85. **TRUE**

86. **FALSE**

87. **TRUE**

88. **C**

89. **B**
    Calley was convicted in 1971 for his part in the 1968 My Lai massacre, where hundreds of Vietnamese civilians were killed.

90. **AIR TRAFFIC CONTROLLERS**

91. **LYNCH**

92. **DUBROFF**

93. **SAVITCH**

94. **HAHN**

95. **McCLURE**

96. **C**

97. **A**

98. **D**

99. **A**

100. **B**

Location
Location
Location

GEOGRAPHY

Location, Location, Location

Every once in a while you've just got to get away from it all. Whether that means jetting to Europe or taking a bus to the other end of town, it helps if you know exactly where you are. You could use a compass or a map, but first, why not take our LOCATION, LOCATION, LOCATION geography quiz? If you close your eyes, you can almost pretend you're there... but that makes it more difficult to answer the questions, of course.

So open your eyes and try out these questions that put the "Gee!" in geography.

CONTINENT #1: ANTARCTICA

Let's take a trip around the globe. We'll start with five questions about the coolest continent on Earth: Antarctica.

1. Antarctica is, on average, the _____ continent on Earth.

    a. windiest
    b. coldest
    c. highest
    d. all of the above

2. The Antarctic Peninsula, which extends north of the Antarctic Circle, is part of:

    a. Antarctica
    b. Chile
    c. the United States
    d. New Zealand

SANDY WOOD & KARA KOVALCHIK

3. Which is true of the Southern Ocean that surrounds Antarctica? It is:

    a. completely frozen year-round
    b. circular in shape
    c. the largest ocean in the world
    d. bordered by every other ocean

4. What country is geographically the closest to the continent of Antarctica?

    a. Australia
    b. New Zealand
    c. South Africa
    d. Chile

5. True or False: The Magnetic South Pole is located on the Antarctic continent.

CONTINENT #2: NORTH AMERICA

Our trip now takes us north of the Equator to North America. Here are five questions about the continent:

6. Lake Nicaragua isn't just the largest lake in Central America, but also the only spot in the world where you can find:

    a. blue pearls
    b. freshwater sharks
    c. poisonous frogs
    d. blind cavefish

7. How many independent countries are located in North America?

    a. 5
    b. 11
    c. 16
    d. 23

8. The river known as the Rio Grande in the United States is known by what name in Mexico?

9. How many U.S. states share a physical border (either by land, river, or lake) with a foreign country?

10. What's the only U.S. state that borders three Canadian provinces?

    a. Alaska
    b. Montana
    c. North Dakota
    d. Minnesota

CONTINENT #3: SOUTH AMERICA

Face it: North America would just be "America" if it weren't for South America. See how well you answer these five questions regarding our continental neighbor.

11. The name of the tallest mountain in South America starts with the same letter as both the mountain range it belongs to and the country in which it lies. What's the letter?

12. What feature makes Bolivia and Paraguay unique among South American nations?

    a. They lie on the Equator.
    b. They share a military force.
    c. They border North America.
    d. They are landlocked.

13. The United Provinces of the Rio de la Plata became what South American nation in 1880?

14. Two of which South American country's major lakes are known by the rather odd names of Poopo and Titicaca?

15. At one point in history, all the lands of South America (except Brazil) and all of Central America and Mexico were collectively known by which name?

    a. Amazonia
    b. New Spain
    c. Magelland
    d. The West Indies

CONTINENT #4: AUSTRALIA

While we're on the south side of the globe, let's slide over (and down under) to the island continent of Australia.

16. The Great Barrier Reef lies in what appropriately named sea?

    a. the Barrier Sea
    b. the Australian Sea
    c. the Queensland Sea
    d. the Coral Sea

17. The antipodal (exact opposite) point on the Earth from the Australian mainland is located:

    a. in Canada
    b. in Alaska
    c. in the Atlantic Ocean
    d. in Greenland

18. True or False: Australia is the world's largest exporter of beef.

19. Australia is home to which of the following?

    a. the Kara Sea
    b. the Great Sandy Desert
    c. both A and B
    d. neither A nor B

20. Long known for its pearls, what small (1 square mile) island off the coast of Australia shares its name with a day of the week?

    a. Saturday Island
    b. Sunday Island
    c. Monday Island
    d. Thursday Island

CONTINENT #5: ASIA

Next, we go to Asia. Despite having the shortest name of any continent, it has one-third of the world's land and nearly two-thirds of Earth's population.

21. China is more properly known as:

    a. The Republic of China
    b. The Communist State of China
    c. The People's Republic of China
    d. none of the above

22. True or False: Measured from sea level, *ALL* of Earth's 50 highest mountains are located in Asia.

23. The entire continent of Asia lies within:
    a. the Northern Hemisphere
    b. the Southern Hemisphere
    c. the Eastern Hemisphere
    d. the Western Hemisphere

24. Areas of three Asian nations spread over into other continents. Which of the following does *not*?
    a. Russia
    b. Papua New Guinea
    c. Egypt
    d. Turkey

25. The total land area of Japan is closest in size to the total land area of which of these U.S. states?
    a. California
    b. Maryland
    c. Alabama
    d. Delaware

CONTINENT #6: AFRICA
To conclude our tour of "A" continents (Antarctica, the Americas, Australia, and Asia), we visit that cradle of civilization, Africa.

26. Africa's Lake Tanganyika holds what superlative among the world's lakes?
    a. deepest
    b. longest
    c. warmest
    d. purest

27. Just as Vatican City is a nation bordered on all sides by Italy, what African nation is bordered on all sides by South Africa?

28. The Orange River was so-named:

   a. because its muddy water is orange
   b. after a Dutch royal family
   c. because it helps water orange groves
   d. for the orangutans that drink from its water

29. The names of what two African nations can be turned into the names of two *other* African nations by adding two letters?

30. True or False: The Equator runs through the African nation known as Equatorial Guinea.

CONTINENT #7: EUROPE

Now we end our whirlwind continent-to-continent extravaganza with a sip of Snapple and a trek across Europe.

31. What's the longest river in Europe?

   a. Danube
   b. Rhine
   c. Thames
   d. Volga

32. True or False: Monaco has the highest population density and smallest land area of any independent state in Europe.

33. What language is the "mother tongue" of more Europeans than any other?

    a. English
    b. German
    c. French
    d. Russian

34. Which of the following was *NOT* a founding member of the European Union?

    a. United Kingdom
    b. Portugal
    c. Spain
    d. all of the above

35. True or False: Europe has a smaller land area than any continent except Antarctica.

AIN'T NO MOUNTAIN HIGH ENOUGH

What is the name of the tallest mountain:

36. east of the Mississippi? _____

37. in the Lower 48 states? _____

38. in Canada?_____

39. in North America?_____

STATELY MANNERS

40. This is the only state in the U.S. with a one-syllable name.

41. Three times in the 20th century, this state's government introduced legislation to reduce the state's name to one word; each time, the motion was defeated.

    a. South Carolina
    b. West Virginia
    c. North Dakota
    d. New Jersey

42. What state leads the nation in the growing of peaches?

    a. California
    b. South Carolina
    c. Georgia
    d. Texas

43. More than 40 percent of all trade between the U.S. and Canada travels through which of these states?

    a. New York
    b. Washington
    c. Minnesota
    d. Michigan

JUST ADD SNAPPLE!

To answer the following question, place the seven letters that make up "SNAPPLE" in the correct blanks:

44. What part of Michigan borders Wisconsin?

    U _ P _ R   _ E _ I N _ U _ _

45. What's the only U.S. state that is home to three cities, each with a population of greater than one million?

    a. New York
    b. Texas
    c. Florida
    d. California

46. What part-island section of southern China reverted to Chinese rule in 1999?

47. Which state is *NOT* part of the western U.S. intersection known as the Four Corners?

    a. Colorado
    b. New Mexico
    c. Arizona
    d. Wyoming

48. In 1949, what became the newest province to join Canada?

    a. Saskatchewan
    b. Newfoundland
    c. Alberta
    d. British Columbia

49. What country is known locally to its inhabitants as Zhong Guo?

AN ELEMENTARY QUIZ

Monkey wrench time! This looks like chemistry, but it isn't... exactly. In the first blank, list the two-letter abbreviation of the chemical element shown. In the second, name the state that uses those two letters as its postal abbreviation. In the example, Aluminum's chemical symbol is AL, which is also the postal abbreviation for Alabama. You figure out the rest.

EXAMPLE: Aluminum = AL = Alabama

50. Molybdenum = ___ = _____

51. Argon = ___ = _____

52. Neon = ___ = _____

53. Cobalt = ___ = _____

54. Manganese = ___ = _____

55. Linguistically, the name of one of these four state capitals doesn't fit in with the other three. Which one, and why?

 a. Jefferson City
 b. Nashville
 c. Montpelier
 d. Indianapolis

56. Alaska, Florida, Idaho, Oklahoma, Texas, and West Virginia are the six U.S. states whose shapes share what physical feature?

57. From what area of New York State does Wendy "The Snapple Lady" Kaufman hail?

    a. Buffalo
    b. The Bronx
    c. Long Island
    d. Poughkeepsie

58. What country produces more cotton, eggs, pigs, potatoes, rice, sheep, tobacco, and wheat than any other?

    a. China
    b. United States
    c. Australia
    d. Russia

TOWN AND COUNTRY

Each entry below is a city in both of the states that appear to the right. Use the "greater than" (>) or "less than" (<) sign to indicate which city has the *larger* population. In the example provided, GA > ME because the population of Augusta, Georgia, is greater than the population of Augusta, Maine.

EXAMPLE: Augusta   GA _>_ ME

59. Charleston   SC ___ WV

60. Pasadena   CA ___ TX

61. Peoria   AZ ___ IL

62. Portland   ME ___ OR

LOCATION, LOCATION, LOCATION: GEOGRAPHY

63. True or False: The Cadillac automobile is named for the founder of Detroit.

64. True or False: Ohio is not only the home of the men credited with the first powered heavier-than-air flight (the Wright brothers) but also the first American in orbit (John Glenn) and the first man on the moon (Neil Armstrong).

65. What's the only Canadian province (not territory!) that borders Alaska?

    a. British Columbia
    b. Saskatchewan
    c. Alberta
    d. Manitoba

66. Identify the location where this flag is flown:

67. What continent was given its name before it was even "discovered" by Europeans?

68. Where would one have to travel to visit Craters of the Moon National Monument?

    a. the North Pole
    b. the Moon
    c. Idaho
    d. Mexico

69. Through World War I, what was the only U.S. National Park located east of the Mississippi River?

    a. Acadia (Maine)
    b. Everglades (Florida)
    c. Great Smoky Mountains (Tenn./N.C.)
    d. Shenandoah (Virginia)

70. The United States is currently the world's third-largest country, measured by:

    a. land area
    b. population
    c. both A and B
    d. neither A nor B

71. What U.S. state has a higher percentage of forest (more than 80 percent) than any other?

    a. Maine
    b. Washington
    c. Minnesota
    d. Delaware

72. Nine of 10 ten top-producing coal mines in the United States are located in:

    a. Pennsylvania
    b. Wyoming
    c. West Virginia
    d. Texas

73. How many U.S. states make up the area commonly known as New England?

74. What animal gave the Canary Islands their name?

75. The Fertile Crescent was an area situated between what two rivers?

    a. Mekong / Red
    b. Danube / Rhone
    c. Euphrates / Tigris
    d. Ganges / Nile

VOWEL OBSTRUCTION

Each of the three answers below contains five missing consonants. Place them in the blanks in the correct order and the answer to each clue will appear.

76. Salt Lake City to certain people, including Roseanne.

    B I _ _ _ _ _ A C E

77. Arkansas is based on a Quapaw word meaning "_____ people."

    D O _ _ _ _ _ E A M

78. Germany, to those who are German.

    D E U _ _ _ _ _ A N D

AN "A" FOR EFFORT

In this quiz, the word(s) in each answer are special in that they contain no vowels *other than* A. You won't find an E, an I, an O, or a U in any of them. We even took out Y, just in case.

79. This country's capital city is Antananarivo:

    _____

80. An island nation east of West Palm Beach, Florida:

    _____

81. This is the second-largest of the former Soviet republics. _____

82. A Moroccan city made famous by the film that shares its name. _____

83. Peter Minuit's famous land acquisition (for 60 gilders): _____

84. What nation bordered only three countries in 1989, but now borders *seven* countries?

85. Mount Rushmore, where four faces are carved into a huge granite cliff, depicts two U.S. presidents from:

    a. the 18th century
    b. the 19th century
    c. the 20th century
    d. none of the above

86. With nearly three-quarters of a million residents, what "C" city is Ohio's largest?

    a. Cleveland
    b. Canton
    c. Cincinnati
    d. Columbus

87. What's the only country whose mainland crosses both the Equator and one of the Tropics?

    a. China
    b. Sudan
    c. Brazil
    d. Indonesia

88. If the oceans were to gradually rise, what would be the first U.S. state to be *completely* submerged underwater?

    a. Delaware
    b. Rhode Island
    c. Florida
    d. Louisiana

89. What's the only U.S. state name that begins with an A but does not end with the same letter?

JUST ADD SNAPPLE!

To answer the following question, place the seven letters that make up "SNAPPLE" in the correct blanks:

90. In 1922, a company purchased the entire 90,000-acre island of Lanai for the sole purpose of growing what fruit?

    _ I _ _ _ _ P _ E _

---

91. True or False: The continent of Asia is home to both the highest point on Earth *and* the lowest spot on Earth.

92. Holland is divided into two provinces, known as:

    a. North Holland and South Holland
    b. Haarlem and The Hague
    c. Burgundy and Hapsburg
    d. Antilles and Aruba

LOCATION, LOCATION, LOCATION, LOCATION: GEOGRAPHY

93. What imaginary line lies at 66° 32′ South latitude?

    a. Tropic of Capricorn
    b. Arctic Circle
    c. Tropic of Cancer
    d. none of the above

94. True or False: Tennessee is bordered by more states (eight) than any other U.S. state.

WAVING GOODBYE

Many states have the typical, boring, symbol-in-the-center-on-a-blue-background flag. Ho-hum. Other states get a bit more creative with their banners, as you'll learn in this quiz.

Name the only U.S. state flag that:

---

95. is green _____

96. has five sides _____

97. was originally square _____

98. depicts the Union Jack _____

99. incorporates the Confederate battle flag

_____

100. features three stars _____

1. **D**
   It also receives less precipitation than any other continent. In fact, most of Antarctica averages about one inch of snow every year. The buildup of snow and ice has taken many centuries.

2. **A**
   By treaty, no individual country owns any part of the continent of Antarctica.

3. **B**
   The Southern Ocean is bounded by the Antarctic Circle, so it is almost completely circular (with the exception of the area interrupted by the Antarctic Peninsula).

4. **D**

5. **FALSE**
   It's located in the Southern Ocean off the coast of East Antarctica, south of Australia.

6. **B**

7. **D**

8. **RIO BRAVO**

9. **17**
   There are 13 states that border Canada (don't forget Alaska!) and four that border Mexico.

10. **B**
    Montana borders (west to east) British Columbia, Alberta, and Saskatchewan.

11. **A**
    The mountain is called Aconcagua; it is part of the Andes, and it's in western Argentina. It's not only the largest mountain in South America, but also in the entire Western Hemisphere.

12. **D**
    All other South American nations border the Atlantic Ocean, Pacific Ocean, or Caribbean Sea.

13. **ARGENTINA**

14. **BOLIVIA**

15. **B**
    At its greatest extent, New Spain also included most of the land surrounding the Gulf of Mexico and the islands in the Caribbean.

16. **D**
    This long group of coral reefs runs for more than 1,200 miles. It's the largest deposit of coral known to exist anywhere in the world.

17. **C**
    Australia fits quite neatly in the Atlantic in an area bordered by North America, South America, and Africa. In fact, Australia and New Zealand are colloquially known as the Antipodes.

18. **TRUE**

19. **B**

20. **D**
    Not quite 2,500 people make Thursday Island their home. The Torres Strait is also home to Tuesday Island, Wednesday Island, and Friday Island.

21. **C**
    The island nation of Taiwan drops the "People's" to become the Republic of China.

22. **TRUE**
    The highest mountain outside of Asia is #57 on the list.

23. C
Mainland Asia is within the Northern Hemisphere, but southern islands considered part of the continent include Indonesia, which crosses below the Equator.

24. B
Only parts of Russia, Turkey, and Egypt are located in Asia.

25. A
Japan's land area (146,000 sq. mi.) is much closer to that of California (159,000 sq. mi.) than to any of the other choices, the largest of which is less than half Japan's size.

26. B
Lake Tanganyika, which borders Tanzania, Burundi, Congo, and Zambia, is the world's longest freshwater lake. It runs north to south approximately 420 miles and averages about 31 miles wide.

27. LESOTHO

28. B
The Orange River and Orange Free State were named after the ruling Dutch family, whose members included William of Orange.

29. MALI (MALAWI) and **NIGER (NIGERIA)**

30. FALSE
The southern border of Equatorial Guinea generally follows the latitude of 1° North.

31. D

32. FALSE
While Monaco's population density is eight times the next-closest European nation, Vatican City (considered a country) is less than one-quarter Monaco's size.

33. D
Estimates show that Russian is the first language of more than 100 million Europeans in Belarus, Russia, and Ukraine. German is second, followed by French and English.

34. D
The original members were Belgium, France, Germany, Italy, Luxembourg, and the Netherlands.

35. FALSE
Antarctica is larger than Europe. Australia is the only continent smaller than Europe.

36. MITCHELL
(North Carolina)

37. WHITNEY
(California)

38. LOGAN
(in the province of Alberta)

39. McKINLEY
(Alaska)

40. MAINE

41. C
Some wish to reduce the name to simply Dakota, but opponents have rejected the idea.

42. A
Georgia, long known as "the Peach State," actually ranks third in peach production behind California and South Carolina.

43. D
The crossing between Detroit, Michigan, and Windsor, Ontario, is the busiest on the U.S.-Canadian border.

44. UPPER PENINSULA

45. B
Houston, Dallas, and
San Antonio

46. MACAO
Hong Kong had already been
taken over by China in 1997.

47. WYOMING
This geographic oddity, in
which four states meet at one
single point, involves Arizona,
Colorado, New Mexico,
and Utah.

48. B
Nunavut was established in
Canada even more recently
(in 1999), but it is considered
a territory, not a province.

49. CHINA

50. MO, MISSOURI

51. AR, ARKANSAS

52. NE, NEBRASKA

53. CO, COLORADO

54. MN, MINNESOTA

55. C
The others end in words
or suffixes that mean "city"
(-polis, -ville).

56. PANHANDLES
All have a thin strip of
land commonly referred to
by that description.

57. C

58. A

59. >

60. >

61. >

62. <

63. TRUE
Antoine de la Mothe Cadillac, a
French explorer, founded Fort
Pontchartrain du Detroit in 1701.

64. TRUE

65. A
Alaska also borders the Yukon
Territory.

66. WASHINGTON, D.C.
It's the official flag of Washington,
D.C., and it is patterned after the
coat of arms used by George
Washington's ancestors.

67. AUSTRALIA
Throughout Europe, there were
stories of an unknown place
called Terra Australis ("land to the
south"). It was first confirmed by
the Dutch in the 17th century.

68. C
The area is covered with cones,
caves, and tubes resembling
those on the lunar surface. Calvin
Coolidge made it a National
Monument in 1924.

69. A

70. C
The United States is the third-
largest country in area (behind
Russia and Canada) and the
third-largest in population
(behind China and India).

71. A
89 percent, according to a
1995 study. North Dakota has
the least, with only 1.0 percent
forested area.

72. B

73. 6

Connecticut, Maine, Massachusetts, New Hampshire, Rhode Island, and Vermont.

74. DOGS

Known as the Island of Dogs (*Insularia Canaria* in Latin), the birds native to the island were later referred to as "canaries."

75. C

76. (BI)RTHPL(ACE)

77. (DO)WNSTR(EAM)

The name applied to the Arkansas River as a major tributary of the Mississippi River.

78. (DEU)TSCHL(AND)

79. MADAGASCAR

80. GRAND BAHAMA

81. KAZAKHSTAN

82. CASABLANCA

83. MANHATTAN

84. POLAND

In 1989, Poland bordered Czechoslovakia, East Germany, and the USSR (none of which now exist). In 2005, its neighbors were Belarus, Czech Republic, Germany, Lithuania, Russia, Slovakia, and Ukraine.

85. B

Jefferson and Lincoln were both 19th-century presidents. The others are Washington (18th century) and Teddy Roosevelt (20th century).

86. D

87. C

The largest South American nation, Brazil extends above the Equator and well south of the Tropic of Capricorn.

88. C

Britton Hill is Florida's highest point, less than 350 feet above sea level.

89. ARKANSAS

The others are Alabama, Alaska, and Arizona.

90. PINEAPPLES

91. TRUE

Both Mount Everest and the Dead Sea are located in Asia.

92. A

93. D

That latitude is better known as the Antarctic Circle. The Tropics lie at 23° 27' latitude (Cancer north, Capricorn south).

94. FALSE

Missouri is also bordered by eight states.

95. WASHINGTON

96. OHIO

97. ALABAMA

98. HAWAII

The Union Jack appears in the canton of Hawaii's flag to honor its past as a British possession.

99. MISSISSIPPI

Georgia's flag also incorporated the Confederate battle flag before a recent series of redesigns.

100. TENNESSEE

4

Chapter & Verse

Literature and
Language

You've bought this book, so we're guessing you can read. Bravo! Chances are you'll do well in CHAPTER AND VERSE. We've got it all covered in this section—from William Shakespeare and Charles Dickens to Fran Drescher and Tom Arnold (yes, they're authors, too!) We'll also have an identity crisis with some comic book heroes, and we'll see if you can avoid being stung by the spelling bee. Get ready! We're going to give your cerebrum a workout.

1. The names of what two Shakespeare characters are part of the NATO alphabet used for radio communication (Alpha, Bravo, Charlie...)?

2. How many syllables are there in the proper pronunciation of the word "mischievous"?

3. According to Greek mythology, how did Paris attack Achilles' heel, thereby killing him?

    a. He sliced it with a sword.
    b. He had his serpent bite it.
    c. He shot it with a poisoned arrow.
    d. He struck it with a hammer.

4. In what language does *once* mean 11?

5. Which of the following was true of Vlad the Impaler, the real person on whom the Dracula legend was based?

    a. He lived in a castle in Transylvania.
    b. He was killed by a stake through the heart.
    c. Others could not see his reflection.
    d. He slept inside a wooden coffin.

6. In American Sign Language, what number is represented by waving a "thumbs-up" sign?

7. What British author became the first editor of *The London Daily News* in 1846?

8. Other authors have since taken over the storyline, but how many books did L. Frank Baum originally write for his *Oz* series?

   a. 3
   b. 7
   c. 14
   d. 38

9. To what was poet F. Gelett Burgess referring when he wrote, "I'd rather see than be one"?

10. Which comedienne described a difficult childhood in her autobiography, *My Life as a Woman*?

    a. Roseanne
    b. Lily Tomlin
    c. Brett Butler
    d. Whoopi Goldberg

SHOOTING BLANKS

The Board of the Modern Library selected its Top 100 English-Language Novels of the 20th Century back in 1998. Using the author's name to help you, fill in the blanks in these titles. You'll need two of the boxes below to complete each one. Two have been used in the example.

ADVENTURES	BRIDGE	GRAPES	PRIME	THE LOCUST
WINGS	AGE	CALL	SAN LUIS REY	
THE MATTER		WRATH	ALL FLESH	DAY
INNOCENCE	THE DOVE	THE WILD	AUGIE MARCH	
DEATH	MISS JEAN BRODIE	THE HEART	WAY	

EXAMPLE: *THE ___GRAPES___ OF ___WRATH___*
by John Steinbeck.

11. *THE _____ OF _____*
by Samuel Butler

12. *THE _____ OF _____*
by Henry James

13. *THE _____ OF _____*
by Thornton Wilder

14. *THE _____ OF _____*
by Graham Greene

15. *THE _____ OF _____*
by Edith Wharton

16. *THE _____ OF _____*
by Nathanael West

17. *THE _____ OF _____*
by Muriel Spark

18. *THE _____ OF _____*
by Saul Bellow

19. *THE _____ OF _____*
by Elizabeth Bowen

20. *THE _____ OF _____*
by Jack London

SPELLBINDING

The answers to these five questions are all words that have been used to win the National Spelling Bee. In true test fashion, you must not only provide the correct answer, but spell it correctly as well. And keep your eyes on your own book (we'll be checking!)

21. Japanese for "divine wind," what eight-letter word originated with the typhoon that saved Japan from certain destruction by repelling the Mongol Navy in 1281?

    _____

22. In the song "All I Want for Christmas Is My Two Front Teeth," what more specific seven-letter word could be used to refer to either of those teeth?

    _____

23. What 11-letter word describes the pigment that gives most forms of plant life a green hue?

    _____

24. On the cover of the Beatles' album *Help!*, the Fab Four can be seen communicating via what visual system using flags (known by a nine-letter word)?

    _____

25. What nine-letter word is a dog breed that shares its name with a state in northern Mexico?

    _____

26. Romance novelist Barbara Cartland was the step-grandmother of what royal figure?

27. Which of the following was *not* the title of a James Michener novel?

    a. *Texas*
    b. *Arizona*
    c. *Alaska*
    d. *Hawaii*

28. What's the name of the newspaper with the largest circulation in the U.S.?

29. A Braille character is composed of a maximum of how many raised dots?

    a. four
    b. six
    c. eight
    d. nine

30. Dr. L.L. Zamenhof, a Polish eye doctor, invented what "universal" language in 1887?

E BEFORE I (DON'T ASK US WHY)

The answers to each of the following literature questions include a word that contradicts the "I before E, except after C" rule. As any good Snapple drinker knows, rules were *made* to be broken.

---

31. What 1911 poem by Rudyard Kipling attempts to explain why males are at a disadvantage?

32. What Samuel Taylor Coleridge poem contains the oft-repeated line, "Water, water everywhere, / Nor any drop to drink"?

33. What Horton Foote screenplay won an Oscar in 1983 (and one for actor Robert Duvall, as well)?

34. In 1929, Robert and Helen Lynd published the renowned *Middletown*, a sociology study involving people in what Indiana city?

35. The Hugo Award is presented annually to writers who excel in what genre?

MASSIVE MASTHEADS

You've got *The New York Times*, *The Chicago Tribune*, and *The Miami Herald*. In many other cases, however, newspapers joined forces over the years and ended up with lengthy, hyphenated names. Here are four examples of major newspapers that match this description. In the blanks provided, name the city in which these papers are published.

36. *THE EXPRESS-NEWS* _____

37. *THE POST-INTELLIGENCER* _____

38. *THE STAR-TELEGRAM* _____

39. *THE UNION-TRIBUNE* _____

STRIKE UP THE BANNED

40. True or False: Through 2005, not a single Stephen King novel has appeared on the ALA's annual list of "100 Most Frequently Challenged Books."

41. True or False: A version of *Little Red Riding Hood* was banned from a California school district for indicating that the girl's basket contained wine.

42. True or False: *The Story of Doctor Dolittle* was banned from some libraries because it included passages during which Polynesia the parrot used some racially-insulting terms.

43. What letter is removed from "vodka" to make the Russian word for water?

44. *Animal Farm's* Boxer was what type of creature?

   a. dog
   b. pig
   c. horse
   d. sheep

45. In what southern state was playwright Tennessee Williams born?

46. Stephen King suffered broken legs in a 1999 car crash. In which of his previous novels did the main character also suffer broken legs in an auto accident?

47. Three men named Robert have been Poet Laureate of the United States. Name any one of them.

WEINERSCHNITZEL!

Okay, we admit it, we like German words. They sound mischievous even if they're not. Following are five German-language words that appear with some regularity in English literature. Match the terms in Column A with the definitions in Column B.

COLUMN A	**COLUMN B**
48. DOPPELGANGER ___	A. counterpart or alter ego
49. LEITMOTIF ___	B. spirit of the times
50. SCHADENFREUDE ___	C. anguish, pessimism
51. ZEITGEIST ___	D. a dominant, recurring theme
52. WELTSCHMERZ ___	E. satisfaction in others' misfortune

53. How is British author Martin Amis related to the late British author Kingsley Amis? Martin is:

   a. his son
   b. his brother
   c. his cousin
   d. no relation

54. What *Winnie the Pooh* character did not appear in A.A. Milne's stories, but was created specifically for the Disney cartoons?

55. What point-size text is the closest equivalent to one inch of vertical space?

56. Which hardcover Dr. Seuss book has sold more copies than any other?

   a. *Green Eggs and Ham*
   b. *Horton Hears a Who*
   c. *How the Grinch Stole Christmas*
   d. *The Cat in the Hat*

57. Fill in the blanks in the titles of these two popular young persons' books by Judy Blume:

   Tales of a Fourth Grade _____

   Are You There, God? It's Me, _____

SHAZAM, SHAZAM, SHAZAM!

Comic book character Captain Marvel received his powers from an Egyptian wizard who channeled them through six historic/mythological figures (whose names begin with S, H, A, Z, A, and M). Match each one in Column A with the corresponding attribute given to the good Captain in Column B.

The last answer is provided to get you started (Mercury = SPEED).

COLUMN A	COLUMN B
58. Solomon	STRENGTH
59. Hercules	STAMINA
60. Achilles	POWER
61. Zeus	WISDOM
62. Atlas	COURAGE
Example: Mercury ⟶	SPEED

63. Each of these four writing "groups" formed in England. Place them in order, in the era they flourished, from oldest to newest:

    - Angry Young Men
    - Bloomsbury Group
    - Graveyard School
    - Pre-Raphaelites

64. Which answer best fits into the blank:

    SNAPPLE is a(n) _____ of *PEN PALS*.

    a. lipogram
    b. palindrome
    c. anagram
    d. none of the above

65. Which of the following entries correctly completes the last part of the title of one of the books in J.K. Rowling's series: *HARRY POTTER AND THE...*?

    - *CHAMBER OF FIRE*
    - *GOBLET OF STONE*
    - *SORCERER'S SECRETS*
    - *HALF-BLOOD PRINCE*
    - *ORDER OF AZKABAN*
    - *PRISONER OF THE PHOENIX*

66. Which of the friends in Ann Brashares's 2001 book, *The Sisterhood of the Traveling Pants*, stayed home for the summer?

    a. Tibby
    b. Lena
    c. Bridget
    d. Carmen

VOWEL OBSTRUCTION

Each of the three answers below contains five missing consonants. Place them in the blanks in the correct order, and the answer to each clue will appear.

67. Subject of Arthur Miller's play, *The Crucible*.

    W I _ _ _ _ _ A F T

68. An adjective meaning "former."

    E _ _ _ _ _ I L E

69. Last name of the philosopher author of *Thus Spake Zarathustra*.

    N I E _ _ _ _ _ E

AN "A" FOR EFFORT

In this quiz, the word(s) in each answer are special in that they contain no vowels *other than* A. You won't find an E, an I, an O, or a U in any of them. We even took out Y, just in case.

70. This Communist author was a foreign correspondent for *The New York Tribune*: _____

71. Decks of these test preparation tools have helped millions learn English: _____

72. This writer is known for his amazing *The Metamorphosis*: _____

73. This 13th-century document is perhaps the most important legislation of its era: _____

74. Joyce Clyde Hall published these, the world's most popular greetings: _____

A STORY TO TELL

Even if you haven't read these five autobiographies, the sentiments in the titles may provide enough clues to help you match them up with their respective authors.

List of Authors:

TOM ARNOLD
GEORGE TAKEI
FRAN DRESCHER
ED McMAHON
MICKEY ROONEY

75. *Enter Whining* _____

76. *For Laughing Out Loud* _____

77. *How I Lost Five Pounds in Six Years* _____

78. *Life Is Too Short* _____

79. *To the Stars* _____

80. Which of the following is the correct spelling of the last name of the author of the *Lord of the Rings* trilogy?

   a. Tolkein
   b. Tolkine
   c. Tolkien
   d. none of the above

81. True or False: The word "tycoon" is based on *taikun*, a title once used by Japanese Shoguns.

82. What American author's unusually titled books include *Mardi, Omoo,* and *Typee*?

   a. Herman Melville
   b. Mark Twain
   c. Philip Roth
   d. Thomas Wolfe

83. True or False: *Call of the Wild* author Jack London ran for mayor of Oakland, California, as a Socialist.

84. What was the name of the "little red-haired girl" on whom Charlie Brown had a crush in the *Peanuts* comic strip?

   a. Violet
   b. Frieda
   c. Peppermint Patty
   d. none of the above

85. What romance writer uses the pseudonym J.D. Robb when writing mysteries?

   a. Nora Roberts
   b. Danielle Steel
   c. LaVyrle Spencer
   d. Fern Michaels

86. How many dots and/or dashes are used to represent each Morse Code number from 1 to 10?

POEM BOHEME

Match the type of poem (in Column A) with the correct number of written lines (Column B).

COLUMN A	COLUMN B
87. CLERIHEW	3 LINES
88. SONNET	4 LINES
89. HAIKU	5 LINES
90. LIMERICK	14 LINES

THE TELL-TALE QUIZ

American poet and writer Edgar Allan Poe has influenced many aspects of pop culture. Here are five examples.

91. First published in *Graham's Magazine,* what Edgar Allan Poe work is popularly considered to be the world's first detective story? _____

92. The Edgar Allan Poe Awards are presented annually to the top writers of what genre?

   a. mystery
   b. horror
   c. poetry
   d. short stories

93. For more than half a century, a mysterious stranger has visited Edgar Allan Poe's grave site (on the writer's birthday) to adorn the plot with what flower-and-booze combination? _____

94. True or False: The NFL's Baltimore Ravens were named for the poem "The Raven," by one of Baltimore's most famous residents, Edgar Allan Poe.

95. What rock group began as a one-off project with the album *Tales of Mystery and Imagination*, filled with musical interpretations of several Edgar Allan Poe tales?

    a. The Jimi Hendrix Experience
    b. The Alan Parsons Project
    c. The George Baker Selection
    d. The Dave Matthews Band

THE LAST WORD

In the following, the last word in the titles of each of these famous books is incorrect. In the blanks provided, list the word that should appear at the end of each title.

96. *LORD OF THE **RINGS*** by WILLIAM GOLDING

    _____

97. *THE SECRET **GARDEN*** by JOSEPH CONRAD

    _____

98. *ALL THE KING'S **HORSES*** by ROBERT PENN WARREN

    _____

99. *A HANDFUL OF **DIRT*** by EVELYN WAUGH

    _____

100. *THE GREAT **SANTINI*** by F. SCOTT FITZGERALD

    _____

1. ROMEO and JULIET

2. THREE
   According to Webster's, the accent is on the first syllable. It's pronounced "miss-che-ves."

3. C

4. SPANISH
   Once is pronounced "ohn-say."

5. A

6. 10

7. CHARLES DICKENS

8. C

9. A PURPLE COW

10. A

11. *WAY, ALL FLESH*

12. *WINGS, THE DOVE*

13. *BRIDGE, SAN LUIS REY*

14. *HEART, THE MATTER*

15. *AGE, INNOCENCE*

16. *DAY, THE LOCUST*

17. *PRIME, MISS JEAN BRODIE*

18. *ADVENTURES, AUGIE MARCH*

19. *DEATH, THE HEART*

20. *CALL, THE WILD*

21. KAMIKAZE
    This word won the Bee in 1993.

22. INCISOR
    This word won the Bee in 1975.

23. CHLOROPHYLL
    This word won the Bee in 1947.

24. SEMAPHORE
    This word won the Bee in 1946.

25. CHIHUAHUA
    This word won the Bee in 1967.

26. PRINCESS DIANA
    Cartland's daughter, Raine, married Diana's father, the eighth Earl Spencer, in 1976.

27. B
    Michener had several successful novels with one-word titles.

28. *USA TODAY*

29. B
    Braille characters are designed two dots wide and three dots tall.

30. ESPERANTO

31. "THE FEMALE OF THE SPECIES"

32. "THE RIME OF THE ANCIENT MARINER"

33. *TENDER MERCIES*

34. MUNCIE

35. SCIENCE FICTION

36. SAN ANTONIO

37. SEATTLE

38. FORT WORTH

39. SAN DIEGO

40. FALSE

41. TRUE

42. TRUE

43. K

The Russian word for water is *voda*.

44. C

45. MISSISSIPPI

Born Thomas Lanier Williams, he got the nickname "Tennessee" in college, when his father was a politician in the Volunteer State.

46. *MISERY*

Unlike the book, however, King wasn't in the vehicle that caused the crash (he was hit by a van while walking).

47. ROBERT PENN WARREN, ROBERT HASS, ROBERT PINSKY

48. A

49. D

50. E

51. B

52. C

53. A

54. GOPHER

55. 72 POINTS

56. A

57. *NOTHING, MARGARET*

58. WISDOM

59. STRENGTH

60. COURAGE

61. POWER

62. STAMINA

63. GRAVEYARD SCHOOL, PRE-RAPHAELITES, BLOOMSBURY GROUP, ANGRY YOUNG MEN

The Graveyard School met in the 18th century; the Pre-Raphaelites were formed in the 19th century; the Bloomsbury Group appeared in the early 20th century; the Angry Young Men came around in the mid-20th century.

64. C

An anagram contains the same letters, but in a different order.

65. *HALF-BLOOD PRINCE*

The others, in their correct sequence, are *Sorcerer's Stone, Chamber of Secrets, Prisoner of Azkaban, Goblet of Fire,* and *Order of the Phoenix.*

66. A
The *Traveling Pants* series has performed quite well despite the sad distinction of a memorable publication date for the first novel: September 11, 2001.

67. (WI)TCHCR(AFT)

68. (E)RSTWH(ILE)

69. (NIE)TZSCH(E)

70. KARL MARX

71. FLASH CARDS

72. FRANZ KAFKA

73. MAGNA CARTA

74. HALLMARK CARDS
Like the male half of your illustrious quizmasters, Joyce Hall was saddled with a name not so commonly used for men.

75. FRAN DRESCHER

76. ED McMAHON

77. TOM ARNOLD

78. MICKEY ROONEY

79. GEORGE TAKEI

80. C
His full name is John Ronald Reuel Tolkien.

81. TRUE

82. A

83. TRUE
He ran for the office in 1901 and again four years later, with little success.

84. D
In the comic strip she was never given a name. In the animated TV special *It's Your First Kiss, Charlie Brown,* she was called Heather.

85. A

86. FIVE
One is dot-dash-dash-dash-dash.

87. 4 LINES

88. 14 LINES

89. 3 LINES

90. 5 LINES

91. THE MURDERS IN THE RUE MORGUE

92. A

93. ROSES and **COGNAC**

94. TRUE

95. B

96. FLIES

97. AGENT

98. MEN

99. DUST

100. GATSBY

The Big Picture

MOVIES

MOVIES

Movies are a lot more than a big tub of popcorn and ringing cell phones. Film is an art form with genres ranging from shoot-em-up action-adventure films and weepy chick flicks to gut-busting comedies and edge-of-your seat dramas. No matter what kind of movies you like to watch, chances are you'll know a lot of the answers in THE BIG PICTURE. Shh! It's starting!

MOVIE MATH MADNESS

Each answer in this quiz is a number. The numerals 1 through 9 will be used in the first nine questions to complete the name of a movie title. Once you're done with those, go down the list vertically, do the math, and place your answer in the last blank. If you add and subtract correctly, the tenth answer should *also* complete a movie's title.

1. _____ *MONTHS*
   plus
2. _____ *DEGREES OF SEPARATION*
   minus
3. _____ *EASY PIECES*
   plus
4. _____ *WEEKS' NOTICE*
   plus
5. _____ *MEN AND A BABY*
   minus
6. _____ *WEDDINGS AND A FUNERAL*
   plus
7. _____ *MEN OUT*
   minus
8. _____ *YEARS IN TIBET*
   plus
9. _____ *CRAZY SUMMER*
   equals
10. _____ *GHOSTS*

11. Clark Gable won an Oscar for his role in which of these 1930s films?

    a. *It Happened One Night*
    b. *Saratoga*
    c. *Gone With the Wind*
    d. *Mutiny on the Bounty*

12. What 1982 film introduced us to a Green Beret survivalist named John?

13. Which of the following did Ernest *not* "go to" in the Jim Varney film series?

    a. camp
    b. jail
    c. work
    d. school

14. True or False: As of the end of 2005, half the films in the all-time U.S. box office Top 10 were sequels.

15. Which of these men was the oldest actor to portray Agent 007 in an official *James Bond* film?

    a. Timothy Dalton
    b. Sean Connery
    c. George Lazenby
    d. Roger Moore

WHO ARE YOU?

BOY	GIGOLO	MAN	OF
DETECTIVE	RAIDER	INTERNATIONAL	
MYSTERY	PET	THIEVES	GENIUS
MALE	OF	PRINCE	TOMB

Use some combination of the words in the 15 boxes above to complete the movie titles associated with the characters listed below. The shaded boxes are used in the example. Not every title will use the same number of words, and each word will only be used once.

EXAMPLE: ACE VENTURA...

PET	DETECTIVE

16. AUSTIN POWERS...

17. DEUCE BIGALOW...

18. JIMMY NEUTRON...

19. LARA CROFT...

20. ROBIN HOOD ...

21. In what year did the zombie film genre gain new life with *Shaun of the Dead, Shadows of the Dead,* and a remake of *Dawn of the Dead?*

   a. 2002
   b. 2003
   c. 2004
   d. 2005

22. Which of the following Lindsay Lohan films was *NOT* a Disney production?

    a. *The Parent Trap*
    b. *Herbie: Fully Loaded*
    c. *Just My Luck*
    d. *Freaky Friday*

23. What singer rode a motorbike in *The Rocky Horror Picture Show*, drove a truck in *Roadie*, and maneuvered a bus in *Spice World*?

    a. Alice Cooper
    b. Meat Loaf
    c. Neil Diamond
    d. John Denver

24. His father was a Canadian mountie and his brother was a member of Canadian Parliament. Name this legally deaf film comedian.

    a. Dave Thomas
    b. Jim Carrey
    c. Mike Myers
    d. Leslie Nielsen

25. A character named Elliot befriends and protects a character not of his species in what fantasy film from 1977?

AN "A" FOR EFFORT

In this quiz, the word(s) in each answer are special in that they contain no vowels *other than* A. You won't find an E, an I, an O, or a U in any of them. We even took out Y, just in case.

26. A not-so-happy 2003 holiday film starring Billy Bob Thornton: _____

27. A 1965 Disney film about D.C., re-made in 1997: _____

28. The first person to win three Oscars for Best Director: _____

29. Sci-fi B-movie parody whose title ends with an exclamation point: _____

30. Semiautobiographical movie written and directed by Bob Fosse: _____

31. What 1984 film about a Soviet invasion of the United States was the first to earn a PG-13 rating?

32. What was the only movie in the *Star Wars* series *NOT* to earn at least $300 million at American theaters?

    a. *Episode V: The Empire Strikes Back*
    b. *Episode II: Attack of the Clones*
    c. *Episode I: The Phantom Menace*
    d. *Episode VI: Return of the Jedi*

33. Shirley Temple, Hollywood's most famous child star, dominated the box office in the 1930s. In 1974 she was appointed American ambassador to which country?

   a. Denmark
   b. Argentina
   c. Czechoslovakia
   d. Ghana

34. While Tom Felton might not be a household name, his face is familiar to millions around the world as the actor who portrays what character in the *Harry Potter* film series?

   a. Rubeus Hagrid
   b. Ron Weasley
   c. Draco Malfoy
   d. Dudley Dursley

35. Following his retirement from show business, film star Omar Sharif began a second career as a master player of what game?

   a. backgammon
   b. bridge
   c. poker
   d. chess

36. When *The Lord of the Rings: The Return of the King* won the Best Picture Oscar, it was the first sequel to secure the award since what 1974 winner?

37. In 2002 and 2003, the Best Supporting Actress Oscar was won by women whose last names begin with the letter Z. Name both of them.

38. The 1927 film *Wings* was the _____ Best Picture Oscar winner.

    a. first one-syllable
    b. first silent
    c. first ever
    d. all of the above

39. What word best completes this analogy?
Anakin Skywalker is to *light saber* as *Eeyore* is to _____.

    a. bow
    b. tail
    c. hoof
    d. Gopher

40. Based on where they were born, which of these actors does *NOT* belong in a group with the other three?

    a. Russell Crowe
    b. Eric Bana
    c. Heath Ledger
    d. Hugh Jackman

TWICE AS NICE

These four actors share a particular Hollywood superlative: Each one won two Academy Awards for Best Supporting Actor within the same decade. Given the name and those two movies, place the correct decade (1920s, 1990s, etc.) for each entry in the blanks provided.

41. Walter Brennan, for *Come and Get It* and *Kentucky:* _____

42. Jason Robards, for *All the President's Men* and *Julia:* _____

43. Anthony Quinn for *Viva Zapata!* and *Lust for Life:*

   _____

44. Peter Ustinov for *Spartacus* and *Topkapi:*

   _____

45. Only two male actors in the 1990s won a pair of acting Oscars. One was Tom Hanks; name the other.

46. The slogan of legendary film studio Metro-Goldwyn-Mayer, *Ars Gratia Artis*, is Latin for:

   a. We give freely.
   b. Lion see, lion do.
   c. Art for art's sake.
   d. Stupid is as stupid does.

47. What film series character can be seen on screen singing lead vocals with the band Ming Tea?

   a. Ernest P. Worrell
   b. Ace Ventura
   c. Deuce Bigalow
   d. Austin Powers

48. Which of the following actors has *never* appeared in a *Star Wars* film wearing a Darth Vader costume?

   a. David Prowse
   b. James Earl Jones
   c. Sebastian Shaw
   d. Hayden Christensen

49. What fictional movie band's catalogue of albums includes *Rock 'n' Roll Creation* and *Shark Sandwich*?

    a. Eddie and the Cruisers
    b. The Oneders
    c. Spiñal Tap
    d. Wyld Stallynz

50. In the 1984 film *Gremlins*, which of these was *NOT* one of the three rules of owning a Mogwai?

    a. Don't get him wet.
    b. Don't let him fall asleep.
    c. Don't feed him after midnight.
    d. Don't expose him to bright light.

SCREEN SONGS

The American Film Institute published a list of the Top 100 Movie Songs of all time. Column A lists five of the songs, while Column B lists the five movies in which those songs appeared. Match the song with its film.

COLUMN A	COLUMN B
EXAMPLE: "MRS. ROBINSON" ⟶ *THE GRADUATE*	
51. "WHITE CHRISTMAS"	A. *A STAR IS BORN*
52. "MOON RIVER"	B. *TITANIC*
53. "MY HEART WILL GO ON"	C. *HOLIDAY INN*
54. "AS TIME GOES BY"	D. *CASABLANCA*
55. "THE MAN THAT GOT AWAY"	E. *BREAKFAST AT TIFFANY'S*

TITLE TRIOS

Column A contains the name of three similarly titled films. Match these movies with their respective stars in Column B.

COLUMN A

56. *THE WEDDING DATE*

57. *THE WEDDING PLANNER*

58. *THE WEDDING SINGER*

COLUMN B

A. MATTHEW McCONAUGHEY

B. ADAM SANDLER

C. DERMOT MULRONEY

We wouldn't leave the women out! Same deal: Column A contains the name of three similarly titled films. Match these movies with their respective stars in Column B.

COLUMN A

59. *BAMBOOZLED*

60. *BEDAZZLED*

61. *BEWITCHED*

COLUMN B

A. ELIZABETH HURLEY

B. NICOLE KIDMAN

C. JADA PINKETT SMITH

VOWEL OBSTRUCTION

Each of the three answers below contains five missing consonants. Place them in the blanks in the correct order and the answer to each clue will appear.

62. Job held by Woody Allen's character in the 1995 film *Mighty Aphrodite*.

S P O _ _ _ _ _ I T E R

63. An adjective used to describe a real-life relationship between film stars.

    O _ _ _ _ _ E E N

64. Last name of Australian director of 1994's *Little Women.*

    A _ _ _ _ _ O N G

THE WIZARD OF OZ

This 1939 film has long been a favorite of young and old alike. This quiz tests your knowledge of all (or at least some) things Oz.

65. We all remember Auntie Em from *The Wizard of Oz,* but what was the name of Dorothy's uncle?

    a. Buck
    b. Hickory
    c. Henry
    d. Zeke

66. In Munchkinland, the Yellow Brick Road spirals alongside a brick road of what color?

    a. red
    b. blue
    c. green
    d. brown

67. Before departing in his hot-air balloon, the Wizard leaves which of these characters in charge of Oz?

    a. Cowardly Lion
    b. Scarecrow
    c. Dorothy
    d. Tin Man

68. True or False: Though ruby slippers were used in the movie (since they were visually more stunning), the original L. Frank Baum story referred to silver shoes.

69. How many of the major actors/actresses in *The Wizard of Oz* portrayed multiple roles?

UNREAL REELS

Disaster is much easier to tolerate when it's on the movie screen (and you've got a Snapple drink and a bag of popcorn within reach). Here are taglines from five well-known disaster flicks. Match them to the correct movies.

70. "HELL, UPSIDE DOWN."   A. *ARMAGEDDON*

71. "NO WAY DOWN, NO WAY OUT."   B. *OUTBREAK*

72. "NOTHING ON EARTH CAN PREPARE YOU." C. *THE POSEIDON ADVENTURE*

73. "THE DARK SIDE OF NATURE."   D. *THE TOWERING INFERNO*

74. "TRY TO REMAIN CALM."   E. *TWISTER*

75. When seen in theaters, what did the second sequels to the scary films *Jaws, Friday the 13th,* and *The Amityville Horror* have in common?

76. Approximately how much did *Star Wars* earn in its first weekend at the box office back in 1977?

    a. $1.5 million
    b. $12 million
    c. $22 million
    d. $46 million

77. Which of these *Purple* films won an Academy Award?

    a. *The Purple Rose of Cairo*
    b. *Purple Rain*
    c. *The Color Purple*
    d. all of the above

78. What motion picture featured the first appearance of Tom Laughlin in his most famous role, that of an ex-Green Beret named Billy Jack?

    a. *Born Losers*
    b. *Johnny Firecloud*
    c. *Walking Tall*
    d. *Billy Jack*

79. What's notably different about *The Last Picture Show, Young Frankenstein,* and *Paper Moon* compared with most other hit films of the 1970s?

THE FINE PRINT

Sure, we go to the movies for the movie. But there are all those little previews and logos and things that show up before and after the on-screen action. This quiz tests your knowledge of those details.

80. THX, a high-fidelity sound system for movie theaters, was the brainchild of what filmmaker, who wrote and directed the creepy *THX-1138*?

   a. Steven Spielberg
   b. George Lucas
   c. Dino De Laurentiis
   d. Stanley Kubrick

81. Before it became PG, this movie rating was previously known as:

   a. GP
   b. Y
   c. T
   d. JH

82. Todd-AO was a film technology company founded by Michael Todd, the former husband of:

   a. Lana Turner
   b. Zsa Zsa Gabor
   c. Elizabeth Taylor
   d. Marilyn Monroe

83. The letters "DD" and "DTS" apply to what aspect of a DVD movie?

   a. sound quality
   b. extra features
   c. screen size
   d. subtitles

84. What character appeared surprised to see lingerers at the very end of the credits of his 1986 film, telling the audience, "It's over. Go home."?

    a. Marty McFly
    b. Crocodile Dundee
    c. Axel Foley
    d. Ferris Bueller

85. The 1980 musical *Shock Treatment* was a sequel (of sorts) to what cult-hit film?

    a. *Heavy Metal*
    b. *The Rocky Horror Picture Show*
    c. *A Clockwork Orange*
    d. *200 Motels*

86. *Season on the Brink*, which premiered in 2002 as ESPN's first original film, told the story of what sports coach?

    a. Joe Torre
    b. Dan Reeves
    c. Bob Knight
    d. Tom Landry

87. The 1988 film *Who Framed Roger Rabbit?* was based on a Gary Wolf book with what slightly different title?

    a. *Who Killed Roger Rabbit?*
    b. *Who Censored Roger Rabbit?*
    c. *Who Is Roger Rabbit?*
    d. *Who Saved Roger Rabbit?*

88. What movie musical included the antics of such oddly named characters as Frenchy, Putzie, and Doody?

89. In which Alfred Hitchcock film did the director make his cameo appearance in a newspaper ad?

90. What 1980 film was the first in nearly half a century to win a Best Picture Oscar *without* winning one for Best Director, Actor, Actress, Supporting Actor, or Supporting Actress?

RATED PC

Here are brief descriptions of five movies in which computer technology played a major role. Name each film.

91. Sandra Bullock becomes the target of an assassin while debugging computer software (1995).

_____

92. Yul Brynner is a bad-man robot bent on attacking tourists in a computerized adult amusement park (1973). _____

93. Kurt Russell receives an electric shock while working on a computer and it goes to his head (1970)._____

94. Jeff Bridges portrays a computer genius who ends up *inside* the operating system (1982).

_____

95. Keanu Reeves returns to America from a trip to Japan with top-secret information in a chip implanted in his head (1995). _____

PICTURES-IN-PICTURES

Column A lists five real Hollywood films. Column B lists five fictional films, each of which were being filmed and/or shown in the plot of a real film in Column A. Match the correct movie in Column B with the numbered entry in Column A.

In the example, *Raving Beauty* was the film-within-a-film seen in *Cecil B. Demented*.

EXAMPLE:

CECIL B. DEMENTED ⟶ *RAVING BEAUTY*

COLUMN A	COLUMN B
96. *AMERICA'S SWEETHEARTS*	*BLUNTMAN AND CHRONIC*
97. *BOWFINGER*	*TIME OVER TIME*
98. *CITIZEN KANE*	*JACK SLATER IV*
99. *THE LAST ACTION HERO*	*CHUBBY RAIN*
100. *JAY AND SILENT BOB STRIKE BACK*	*TIME ON THE MARCH*

1. 9

2. 6

3. 5

4. 2

5. 3

6. 4

7. 8

8. 7

9. 1

10. 13

11. A

12. *FIRST BLOOD*
Rambo was the title of the second film in the series.

13. C

14. **TRUE**
They were: *Shrek 2*, two *Star Wars* films (*The Phantom Menace* and *Revenge of the Sith*), *The Lord of the Rings: The Return of the King,* and *Spider-Man 2*.

15. D
Roger Moore is three years older than Sean Connery. He was 57 when he starred in his last 007 film, *A View to a Kill.*

16. *INTERNATIONAL MAN OF MYSTERY*

17. *MALE GIGOLO*

18. *BOY GENIUS*

19. *TOMB RAIDER*

20. *PRINCE OF THIEVES*

21. C

22. C

23. B

24. D

25. *PETE'S DRAGON*
Another film with a similar plot but a later release date (1982) was *E.T., the Extra-Terrestrial.*

26. *BAD SANTA*

27. *THAT DARN CAT*
"D.C." was the nickname of the feline, an abbreviation for "Darn Cat."

28. **FRANK CAPRA**
He won for *It Happened One Night, Mr. Deeds Goes to Town*, and *You Can't Take It With You.*

29. *MARS ATTACKS!*

30. *ALL THAT JAZZ*

31. *RED DAWN*

32. A

33. D
President Gerald Ford appointed her ambassador to the Republic of Ghana. In 1989 President George Bush appointed her ambassador to Czechoslovakia.

34. C

35. B

36. *THE GODFATHER: PART II*

37. CATHERINE ZETA-JONES and **RENÉE ZELLWEGER**

38. D

39. B
Just as Skywalker often loses his weapon, Eeyore has a habit of leaving his tail behind.

40. A
Russell Crowe was born in New Zealand; the others were all born in Australia.

41. 1930s
He won a third Best Supporting Actor award in the 1940s.

42. 1970s

43. 1950s

44. 1960s

45. KEVIN SPACEY

46. C

47. D

48. B
While James Earl Jones provided the voice of the Dark Lord, he did not play the role on screen in any of the six films in the series.

49. C
In the 1984 mockumentary, the band's new album is titled *Smell the Glove*.

50. B

51. C

52. E

53. B

54. D

55. A

56. C

57. A

58. B

59. C

60. A

61. B

62. (SPO)RTSWR(ITER)

63. (O)FFSCR(EEN)

64. (A)RMSTR(ONG)

65. C

66. A

67. B

68. TRUE

69. 5
The five were: Ray Bolger (as Hunk and the Scarecrow), Jack Haley (as Hickory and the Tin Man), Margaret Hamilton (as Miss Gulch and the Wicked Witch), Burt Lahr (as Zeke and the Cowardly Lion), and Frank Morgan (as the Coachman, the Doorman, the Guard, Professor Marvel, and the Wizard).

70. C

71. D

72. A

73. E

74. B

75. **THEY WERE ALL SHOWN IN 3-D**
Movie fans, ever-hungry for realistic action, unfortunately failed to find any while viewing these in-your-face movies.

76. A
Amazingly, on its way to becoming the second-biggest movie in U.S. history, the first weekend of receipts totaled only a little over $1.5 million.

77. B
Purple Rain won an Oscar for Best Original Song. The other Purple films mentioned were "skunked" at the Academy Awards.

78. A

79. **ALL WERE SHOT IN BLACK AND WHITE**

80. B

81. A

82. C

83. A
"DD" stands for Dolby Digital; "DTS" means Digital Theater Systems.

84. D

85. B
While the film's setting (Denton) and two of the main characters (Brad and Janet) are the same, much is different in this Richard O'Brien sequel.

86. C

87. B

88. *GREASE*

89. *LIFEBOAT*
In 1944's *Lifeboat*, Hitchcock set the film in a small boat. The problem of how to accomplish his trademark cameo appearance was solved by use of the newspaper ad… for a weight loss product.

90. *CHARIOTS OF FIRE*

91. *THE NET*

92. *WESTWORLD*

93. *THE COMPUTER WORE TENNIS SHOES*

94. *TRON*

95. *JOHNNY MNEMONIC*

96. *TIME OVER TIME*

97. *CHUBBY RAIN*

98. *TIME ON THE MARCH*

99. *JACK SLATER IV*

100. *BLUNTMAN AND CHRONIC*

The Small
Screen

TELEVISION

TELEVISION

Click the "off" button on your remote and flip through the channels of your mind to find the answers to the best questions about television in our **SMALL SCREEN** section. Our questions run the gamut from South Fork to *South Park*, from *Mr. Ed* to Mr. Big. And the best part is there are no commercials!

A VERY BRADY ANALOGY QUIZ

Using the Bradiest section of your brain, choose the answer that best completes each of the following analogies.

1. PETER is to ARTHUR as ALICE is to _____.

   a. Sam
   b. Emma
   c. Kay
   d. Carol

2. GREG is to WESTDALE as CINDY is to_____.

   a. Fillmore
   b. Clinton
   c. Washington
   d. Lincoln

3. BOBBY is to JOE NAMATH as MARCIA is to

   _____.

   a. Warren Melaney
   b. Johnny Bravo
   c. Davy Jones
   d. Billie Jean King

4. BRADY BOYS are to TIGER as BRADY GIRLS are to _____.

   a. Kitty Carry-All
   b. Cousin Oliver
   c. Twinkles
   d. Fluffy

5. GARY COLE is to ROBERT REED as _____ is to FLORENCE HENDERSON.

   a. Shelley Long
   b. Michelle Pfeiffer
   c. Jean Smart
   d. Goldie Hawn

BEAM ME UP, SCOTTY!

6. What TV show's 1964 debut episode was titled "The Vulcan Affair"?

7. What TV show's theme song was "Final Frontier"?

8. For what TV show did William Shatner win his first Emmy award?

MTV SHOWS

Appropriate to the title, this section is not only about original MTV shows but also each answer in this section contains the letter M. Place the correct letters in the blanks to answer the questions.

9. The MTV reality show *I Want a* _____ *Face* featured folks who underwent extensive plastic surgery in hopes of enhancing their resemblance to a celebrity:

   _ _ M _ _ _

10. Which of Sharon and Ozzy's daughters chose not to appear on *The Osbournes*?

    _ _ M _ _

11. Each daughter had her own MTV show, produced by "Papa Joe." What's this family's name?

    _ _ M _ _ _ _

12. Season Five of *The Real World* took place in what U.S. city?

    _ _ _ M _

13. What type of *Control* does Pierre Bouvier exercise on MTV?

    _ _ M _ _ _

14. Which pair best completes this analogy?

    Andy Griffith is to Andy Taylor as _____ is to _____.

    a. Cliff Huxtable, Bill Cosby
    b. Mary Tyler Moore, Mary Richards
    c. Tony Banta, Tony Micelli
    d. Andy Kaufman, Andy Dick

15. Best known as a comedian, who won three consecutive Best Drama Actor Emmy awards in 1966, '67, and '68?

16. What reality show has been around since 1989, without the benefit of any regularly recurring participants?

17. Which of these was a spin-off of Home Box Office?

    a. Showtime
    b. Starz
    c. Cinemax
    d. The Movie Channel

18. Name the first television miniseries, which premiered on ABC in 1976 (hint: the title begins with the letter R).

19. Which of the following do late comedian Rodney Dangerfield and late sports announcer Howard Cosell have in common?

    a. same last name
    b. same birthplace
    c. same birthdate
    d. none of the above

20. In the world of television, Eric, Benjamin, Joseph, and Adam were collectively known as:

21. What Oscar-nominated actor locked horns with "Snapple Lady" Wendy Kaufman on the VH1 reality series *Celebrity Fit Club 2*?

22. The actor who played what *Leave It to Beaver* character grew up to become an L.A. policeman?

    a. Wally Cleaver
    b. Lumpy Rutherford
    c. Eddie Haskell
    d. Gilbert Bates

23. In what country was *CHiPs* star Erik Estrada born?

    a. U.S.
    b. Panama
    c. Cuba
    d. Mexico

24. In the 1969 TV special of the same name, *Frosty the Snowman* mistakenly used what personal greeting?

    a. Happy Thanksgiving!
    b. Happy Birthday!
    c. Happy Halloween!
    d. Happy Gilmore!

25. How many sets of twins lived in the *Full House* household?

26. Every episode of which of these TV shows was filmed in color?

    a. *The Beverly Hillbillies*
    b. *Bewitched*
    c. *Green Acres*
    d. *Gilligan's Island*

CITYSCOPE

The three television shows in each group were set in the same U.S. metropolitan area. Name the cities.

27. *Home Improvement / Martin / Sister, Sister*

    _____

28. *Amen / Strong Medicine / Thirtysomething*

    _____

29. *Good Times* / *Married... With Children* /
    The Bob Newhart Show

    _____

30. *Ally McBeal* / *Crossing Jordan* / *Spenser: For Hire*

    _____

31. *Charmed* / *Dharma and Greg* / *Full House*

    _____

32. What was the very first program broadcast on
    NBC when the network premiered its daily
    schedule back in 1939?

    a. a Dodgers-Giants baseball game
    b. the World's Fair opening ceremony
    c. an interview with the *Gone With the Wind* cast
    d. Franklin D. Roosevelt news conference

33. Which of the following actors did *NOT* appear on
    every episode of *Cheers* during the sitcom's
    eleven-year run?

    a. George Wendt (Norm)
    b. Ted Danson (Sam)
    c. Rhea Perlman (Carla)
    d. John Ratzenberger (Cliff)

34. How many TV stations were licensed by the FCC
    from 1949-52, when the medium first began to
    catch on with the American public?

    a. none
    b. 32
    c. 219
    d. 1,300

35. First broadcast in 1956, *The Huntley-Brinkley Report* was the name of what TV network's evening news program?

    a. ABC
    b. CBS
    c. NBC
    d. DuMont

36. Which of these stars of TV's *M*A*S*H* did not go by a stage name?

    a. Alan Alda
    b. Harry Morgan
    c. Loretta Swit
    d. Jamie Farr

SPINNING OFF

37. Which character from *The Mary Tyler Moore Show* did not star in his or her own spin-off show?

    a. Rhoda Morgenstern
    b. Phyllis Lindstrom
    c. Ted Baxter
    d. Lou Grant

Properly place these four TV shows into the grid below, following the flow of the original show, its spin-offs, and the secondary spin-off.

All in the Family / Good Times / The Jeffersons / Maude

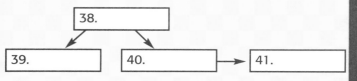

38.

39.   40.   →   41.

MIX AND *M*A*S*H*

Place the names of these characters from TV's *M*A*S*H* correctly into the equation below, showing the order in which they appeared or disappeared from the show. A minus sign indicates a character who left and a plus sign indicates one who was added to the cast. (Colonel Henry Blake was the first major character removed from the cast.)

Names to add:

BURNS	HUNNICUT	McINTYRE
O'REILLY	POTTER	WINCHESTER

	−	BLAKE	
42.	−	_____	
43.	+	_____	
44.	+	_____	
45.	−	_____	
46.	+	_____	
47.	−	_____	= THE END!

48. Ken Jennings' record *Jeopardy!* run in 2004 bettered a record set by Tom McKee, who appeared on 46 consecutive episodes of what game show in 1980?

49. Cable television, first launched in the 1940s, was initially designed to provide programming to:
    a. tall buildings
    b. rural areas
    c. mountainous locations
    d. schools

50. Which of these cable TV stations premiered first?

    a. CNN (Cable News Network)
    b. HSN (Home Shopping Network)
    c. MTV (Music Television)
    d. C-SPAN (Cable-Satellite Public Affairs Network)

51. Place the four stars of *I Love Lucy* (Lucille Ball, Desi Arnaz, Vivian Vance, and William Frawley) in age order from youngest to oldest.

52. The last episode of which one of these four shows was originally seen by an incredible 100 million viewers in the United States?

    a. *Friends*
    b. *The Fugitive*
    c. *M*A*S*H*
    d. *Seinfeld*

53. Which answer best completes this analogy?

    THE SIMPSONS is to *ITCHY AND SCRATCHY* as *SOUTH PARK* is to:

    a. *Bitchy and Slappy*
    b. *Terrance and Phillip*
    c. *Snotley and Booger*
    d. *Timmy and Jimmy*

54. Which of the following was *not* one of the Bradley sisters on *Petticoat Junction?*

    a. Betty Jo
    b. Brenda Jo
    c. Bobbie Jo
    d. Billie Jo

55. The initials D.J., used by the Conners' third-born on TV's *Roseanne,* stood for:

    a. Donna Jennifer
    b. Daniel Junior
    c. David Jacob
    d. Deborah Julie

56. True or False: Every female relative of Samantha who appeared on TV's *Bewitched* had a name ending with the letter A.

57. In the fifth episode of *The Sopranos*, Tony reluctantly had to "silence" an informant while accompanying his daughter to:

    a. a friend's wedding
    b. visit a college campus
    c. a Broadway show
    d. a women's basketball game

WHAT A CHARACTER

In this quiz, you'll identify the names of the actors who played these five famous TV characters. We've given you the list of actors:

CLIFF ARQUETTE	BILL DANA	DON NOVELLO
MURRAY LANGSTON		PAUL REUBENS

58. PEE-WEE HERMAN _____

59. CHARLEY WEAVER _____

60. JOSE JIMINEZ _____

61. THE UNKNOWN COMIC _____

62. FATHER GUIDO SARDUCCI _____

STATION-ARY

Each TV show character in Column A works at a fictitious TV station. In Column B is a list of the call letters of those stations, along with the job the character held. Match the choices in Column B with the ones in Column A.

COLUMN A

COLUMN B

63. MARY RICHARDS
(The Mary Tyler Moore Show)

A. WBJX, Channel 9
sportscaster

64. GEORGE PAPADOPOLIS
(Webster)

B. WPIV, Channel 8
talk show host

65. DICK LOUDON
(The Newhart Show)

C. WJM, Channel 12
assistant producer

66. JOANNIE BRADFORD
(Eight Is Enough)

D. WKS, Channel 3
manager

67. STEVEN KEATON
(Family Ties)

E. KTNS, Channel 8
reporter

VOWEL OBSTRUCTION

Each of the three answers below contains five missing consonants. Place them in the blanks in the correct order and the answer to each clue will appear.

68. James Franciscus starred in this 1971-72 TV series.

L O _ _ _ _ _ E E T

69. The Rabbit and The Houdini were brands of these advertised on TV.

    C O _ _ _ _ _ E W S

70. Maiden name of *The Golden Girls'* Rose Nylund.

    L I _ _ _ _ _ O M

AN "A" FOR EFFORT

In this quiz, the word(s) in each answer are special in that they contain no vowels *other than* A. You won't find an E, an I, an O, or a U in any of them. We even took out Y, just in case.

71. Jim Perry hosted the original NBC version of this TV game show in 1978: _____

72. The early-1960s slogan for Winston cigarettes was criticized for its: _____

73. This now-cancelled soap opera won Best Drama Daytime Emmy awards in 1988, '89, and '90:

    _____

74. This Frat Pack actor's band, Tenacious D, was the subject of an HBO series: _____

75. What *Tiny Toons Adventures* bunny was known by the nickname Babs? _____

MY FRIENDS CALL ME...

Some TV characters' nicknames become so popular that they're rarely referred to by anything else. Here are 10 actors, along with the nickname of their character and the show on which they appeared. Provide the full name of the corresponding character.

To help you along, here's a list of the answers that will appear:

ERWIN HANDLEMAN	FRANCES LAWRENCE	DAISY MAE MOSES	ERNIE PANTUSSO	SAMUEL POWERS
CLARENCE RUTHERFORD	BURL SMITH	CHARLES THATCHER	WARREN WEBER
DOROTHY RAMSEY	CLARENCE RUTHERFORD	BURL SMITH	CHARLES THATCHER	WARREN WEBER

EXAMPLE: Dan Blocker as Hoss on *Bonanza*:
<u>ERIC CARTWRIGHT</u>

76. Nicholas Colasanto as Coach on *Cheers*

_____

77. Chris Burke as Corky on *Life Goes On*

_____

78. Sally Field as Gidget on *Gidget*

_____

79. Fred Grandy as Gopher on *The Love Boat*

_____

80. Irene Ryan as Granny on *The Beverly Hillbillies*

_____

81. Frank Bank as Lumpy on *Leave It to Beaver*

_____

82. Anson Williams as Potsie on *Happy Days*

_____

83. Dustin Diamond as Screech on *Saved By the Bell*

   _____

84. Marc Price as Skippy on *Family Ties*

   _____

85. Kim Fields as Tootie on *The Facts of Life*

   _____

SHE'S A BEAUTY

Following is a list of eight beauty queens along with the roles and TV shows that made them famous. While all of these women won local pageants, only four of them went on to compete for Miss America. Identify those four and place them in the correct blanks.

LONI ANDERSON, Jennifer on *WKRP in Cincinnati*
PRISCILLA BARNES, Terri on *Three's Company*
DELTA BURKE, Suzanne on *Designing Women*
DONNA DOUGLAS, Elly May on *The Beverly Hillbillies*
SHIRLEY JONES, Shirley (the mom) on *The Partridge Family*
CLORIS LEACHMAN, Phyllis on *The Mary Tyler Moore Show*
LEE MERIWETHER, Betty on *Barnaby Jones*
DAWN WELLS, Mary Ann on *Gilligan's Island*

86. Miss Chicago*, 1946: _____

87. Miss California, 1955: _____

88. Miss Nevada, 1960: _____

89. Miss Florida, 1976: _____

   * NOTE: In earlier Miss America pageants, both states *and* large cities were represented by their own contestants.

90. What pre-Brat Pack actress was given the axe (along with several others) after the first season of TV's *The Facts of Life*?

    a. Ally Sheedy
    b. Demi Moore
    c. Molly Ringwald
    d. Mare Winningham

91. Sure, *The Flintstones* lived in Bedrock. Where did *The Jetsons* live?

    a. Marsville
    b. Sky Valley
    c. Orbit City
    d. Comet Corners

92. What name best completes this analogy?

    VANNA WHITE is to *PAT SAJAK* as *SUSAN STAFFORD* is to _____.

93. True or False: In August 2005, New York City police arrested a TV extra for having an NYPD police uniform (used in a role) in his possession.

94. True or False: Paul Sorvino left the cast of *Law & Order* after a season and a half because he didn't enjoy the cold New York weather, which was rough on his singing voice.

95. Name the TV character who succinctly ordered his favorite drink using only four words: "Tea. Earl Grey. Hot."

    a. Giles French *(Family Affair)*
    b. Dick Solomon *(Third Rock From the Sun)*
    c. Jean-Luc Picard *(Star Trek: The Next Generation)*
    d. Cosmo Kramer *(Seinfeld)*

96. Which of Harry Shearer's voices on TV's *The Simpsons* did he name as the most difficult, claiming it required "lots of tea and honey"?

    a. Montgomery Burns
    b. Ned Flanders
    c. Principal Skinner
    d. Waylon Smithers

97. What unfortunate TV record is held by Sonja Christopher?

98. Which of the following was not an item of clothing that was referenced in an episode of *Seinfeld?*

    a. puffy sleeves
    b. manssiere
    c. vacuum pants
    d. urban sombrero

99. Which of these D-titled television shows ran for 452 episodes, more than any other?

    a. *Death Valley Days*
    b. *Dragnet*
    c. *Dynasty*
    d. *Dallas*

100. Who has appeared as a semi-regular correspondent on *The Today Show* for the most number of years?

    a. Gene Shalit, critic
    b. Willard Scott, weather
    c. Rona Barrett, gossip
    d. Jill Rappaport, entertainment

1. **B**

   In one episode, Peter found he had a look-alike named Arthur Owen (with both roles played by Chris Knight). Alice's Cousin Emma appeared in a different episode. She looked identical to housekeeper Alice (with both roles played by Ann B. Davis).

2. **B**

   The older kids (including Greg) attended Westdale High; the middle ones went to Fillmore Junior High; the youngest (including Cindy) attended Clinton Elementary.

3. **C**

   Just like Bobby bragged that he knew Joe Namath (but didn't), Marcia mouthed off about her closeness to Davy Jones. Both Brady kids ended up meeting their heroes before the end of the respective episodes.

4. **D**

   The boys' dog was named Tiger; the girls' cat was named Fluffy. Neither were seen after the series' first few episodes.

5. **A**

   In the Brady films, Gary Cole portrayed father Mike Brady, played by Robert Reed on TV. Likewise, Shelley Long portrayed mother Carol Brady, a role held by Florence Henderson on the sitcom.

6. *THE MAN FROM U.N.C.L.E.*

7. *MAD ABOUT YOU*

8. *THE PRACTICE*

   Shatner won the award for a 2003 guest appearance.

9. *FAMOUS*

10. AIMEE

11. SIMPSON

12. MIAMI

13. *DAMAGE*

14. **B**

    The analogy is real name : character's name in a TV show.

15. BILL COSBY (for *I SPY*)

16. *COPS*

17. C

18. *RICH MAN, POOR MAN*

19. **A**

    They were both born with the last name Cohen.

20. **THE CARTWRIGHTS (from *BONANZA*)**

    The father was Ben and the sons (from oldest to youngest) were Adam, Eric (Hoss), and Little Joe.

21. **GARY BUSEY**

22. **C**

    Ken Osmond played the role of Eddie Haskell.

23. **A**

    He's a native of New York.

24. B

25. **ONE**

    While Michelle Tanner was portrayed by twins, she was only one character on the show. The twins in the show were Alex and Nicky Katsopolis.

26. C

27. DETROIT

28. PHILADELPHIA

29. CHICAGO

30. BOSTON

31. SAN FRANCISCO

32. B

33. D

34. A

While the FCC tried to figure out how to handle overlapping geographic areas, they suspended licensing during this period (although 50+ stations that had already been licensed began broadcasting during this time period).

35. C

36. C

Alda was born Alphonso D'Abruzzo; Harry Morgan's real name is Harold Bratsburg; Jamie Farr was born Jameel Farah.

37. C

38. *ALL IN THE FAMILY*

39. *THE JEFFERSONS*

40. *MAUDE*

41. *GOOD TIMES*

42. McINTYRE

43. HUNNICUT

44. POTTER

45. BURNS

46. WINCHESTER

47. O'REILLY

48. *TIC-TAC-DOUGH*

49. B

Cable TV was originally intended to send signals to rural areas where no broadcast towers were located.

50. D

C-SPAN hit the airwaves in 1979, CNN in 1980, MTV in 1981, and HSN in 1985.

51. ARNAZ, BALL, VANCE, and FRAWLEY

Arnaz was born in 1917, Ball in 1911, Vance in 1909, and Frawley in 1887.

52. C

53. B

Like the youngsters on *The Simpsons* who watch a cartoon titled *Itchy and Scratchy*, the kids in *South Park* are entertained by their favorite cartoon, *Terrance and Phillip*.

54. B

55. C

56. TRUE

They include her aunts Clara, Bertha, Hagatha, and Enchantra, cousin Serena, mother Endora, and daughter Tabitha.

57. B

58. PAUL REUBENS

59. CLIFF ARQUETTE

60. BILL DANA

61. MURRAY LANGSTON

62. DON NOVELLO

63. C

64. A

65. B

66. E

67. D

68. *(LO)NGSTR(EET)*

69. (CO)RKSCR(EWS)

70. (LI)NDSTR(OM)

71. *CARD SHARKS*

72. BAD GRAMMAR
"Winston tastes good like a cigarette should," it was said, was incorrectly phrased. "...As a cigarette should" is the preferred version.

73. *SANTA BARBARA*

74. JACK BLACK
The 1999 HBO series *Tenacious D* lasted only three episodes.

75. BARBARA ANN

76. ERNIE PANTUSSO

77. CHARLES THATCHER

78. FRANCES LAWRENCE

79. BURL SMITH

80. DAISY MAE MOSES

81. CLARENCE RUTHERFORD

82. WARREN WEBER

83. SAMUEL POWERS

84. ERWIN HANDLEMAN

85. DOROTHY RAMSEY

86. CLORIS LEACHMAN

87. LEE MERIWETHER
Meriwether is the only one on the list who went on to win the title of Miss America.

88. DAWN WELLS

89. DELTA BURKE
Since *Designing Women* was set in Georgia, she was referred to in the show as a former "Miss Georgia World" winner.

90. C
It proved a blessing in disguise, as she had a blossoming film career long before *The Facts of Life* cast went shark-jumping in Australia.

91. C

92. CHUCK WOOLERY
Vanna White turns the letters on TV's *Wheel of Fortune* while Pat Sajak hosts. When the show premiered, Susan Stafford worked the board while Chuck Woolery handled the big wheel.

93. TRUE
The Screen Actors Guild immediately issued an alert that actors in New York should refrain from purchasing or transporting police costumes.

94. TRUE
The opera-singing Sorvino was replaced by Jerry Orbach, who (oddly enough) was a trained singer as well.

95. C

96. A

97. SHE IS THE FIRST PERSON EVER VOTED OFF *SURVIVOR*

98. C
Vacuum pants appeared on an episode of *The Golden Girls*.

99. A
Dragnet ran for 430 episodes (combined total of the show's four TV versions). *Dallas* ran for 356 episodes. *Dynasty* ran for 218 episodes.

100. A
Gene Shalit has appeared on the show since 1973.

Sound Off

MUSIC

Whether you're a head banger, a hip hopper, a country crooner, or an opera aficionado, the rhythm, and this SOUND OFF section, is gonna get 'cha. It's a music lover's paradise! After all, where else can Snoop Dogg and Schubert rub elbows?

Now start composing.

VOWEL OBSTRUCTION

Each of the three answers below contains five missing consonants. Place them in the blanks in the correct order and the answer to each clue will appear.

1. Formed in London in 1977, this was one of the first all-women hardrock bands.

    G I _ _ _ _ _ O O L

2. Type of "Men" that Status Quo sang about in their lone 1968 hit.

    M A _ _ _ _ _ I C K

3. Dexter Holland's band, whose hits included "I Choose" in 1997 and "Can't Repeat" in 2005.

    O _ _ _ _ _ I N G

4. Despite his many name changes, Prince did have a real first name once. What was it?

5. Which of these four values is wrong?

   In the year ___A___, the Live Aid concerts were held in ___B___ and ___C___ to benefit ___D___.

   a. A = 1985
   b. B = New York
   c. C = London
   d. D = Ethiopia

6. Which member of the Brat Pack was married to singer/choreographer/*American Idol* judge Paula Abdul for two tumultuous years?

   a. Rob Lowe
   b. Emilio Estevez
   c. Judd Nelson
   d. Andrew McCarthy

7. In modern music, what part of a drum kit provides the backbeat?

   a. bass
   b. tom
   c. snare
   d. kettle

8. True or False: "I'm a Little Teapot" was a children's song written by an 18th-century British schoolteacher to entertain the students in her classroom.

JUST ADD SNAPPLE!
To answer the following question, place the seven letters that make up "SNAPPLE" in the correct blanks:

9. Spinderella served as DJ for what rap act?

   _ _ _ T - _ - _ _ _ A

SCANDALOUS GIRLS

Match the "bad girl" in Column A with the associated scandal in Column B.

COLUMN A	COLUMN B
10. Christina Aguilera	A. Super Bowl XXXVIII "wardrobe malfunction"
11. Janet Jackson	B. 55-hour marriage annulled in 2004
12. Beyoncé Knowles	C. Madonna removed her garter at the 2004 VMAs
13. Jennifer Lopez	D. Her father/manager was sued for wasting $32 million
14. Britney Spears	E. See-through scarf (er, dress) at 2000 Grammy Awards

15. Which of the following composers did *NOT* live in the 20th century?

   a. Schubert
   b. Schoenberg
   c. Strauss
   d. Stravinsky

16. Name the performers who held the top five positions on the pop music chart the week of April 4, 1964.

17. In 2001, what U.S. city changed the name of Shallowford Road to Usher Raymond Parkway in honor of the R&B vocalist born and raised there?

18. Which Gibb brother was *NOT* a member of the Bee Gees?

    a. Andy
    b. Barry
    c. Maurice
    d. Robin

19. What country-rock band favored album titles beginning with the letter H, such as *Harbor, Hideaway,* and *History?*

    a. The Eagles
    b. America
    c. Pure Prairie League
    d. Lynyrd Skynyrd

20. Which of the following musical acts did *NOT* have a Top-20 hit with a song titled "Baby, I Love Your Way"?

    a. Big Mountain
    b. Will to Power
    c. Eurythmics
    d. Peter Frampton

PLAYING CARDS AND MUSIC

Popular music has always had its pulse on poker. There's the album *Full House*, the hit "Queen of Hearts," and even singer Ben Folds (okay, that last one's a stretch). Here are five questions representing a Royal Flush of 10, J, Q, K, and A. Just pretend they're all the same suit. (Hey, if you're gonna dream, dream big.)

21. ***Ten***, the platinum-selling debut album by Pearl Jam, included how many tracks (in contrast to its title)?

    a. 3
    b. 8
    c. 11
    d. 16

22. **Jack** White of the White Stripes is what relation to bandmate Meg White?

    a. father
    b. ex-husband
    c. cousin
    d. brother

23. **Queen** embarked on a concert tour in 2005 for the first time in nearly 20 years. What guest vocalist filled in for the late Freddie Mercury?

    a. Chris Thompson
    b. Paul Rodgers
    c. George Michael
    d. Robbie Williams

24. **"King** Tut" became a Top-20 novelty hit back in 1978 for what funnyman (backed by his band, the Toot Uncommons)?

    a. Steve Martin
    b. Eddie Murphy
    c. "Weird Al" Yankovic
    d. Rick Dees

25. **Ace** of Base formed in 1990 in what European country?

    a. Netherlands
    b. Austria
    c. Ireland
    d. Sweden

26. What founding member of Pink Floyd was born with the first name Roger?

27. Tupac Shakur got his start in the professional music business as a roadie and dancer for what rap group of the 1990s?

    a. Digital Underground
    b. Boogie Down Productions
    c. Arrested Development
    d. Public Enemy

28. What #2 hit single by Survivor was the theme song from the motion picture *Rocky IV*?

29. What chart-topping 1982 instrumental piece by Evangelos Odyssey Papathanassiou was initially titled simply "Titles"?

30. In interviews, Robert Plant pointed out that the proper pronunciation of the title of the Led Zeppelin song "D'yer Mak'r" rhymes with the name of what country?

31. Three Top-40 hits recorded by Glen Campbell mention U.S. cities. Name one of them.

32. What odd title did the Traveling Wilburys give their second album?

   a. *Debut*
   b. *TW4*
   c. *On Sale*
   d. *Volume III*

EVERYWHERE A SIGN

Match the following musical notations in Column A with the symbols they most resemble in Column B.

COLUMN A		COLUMN B
33. flat	A.	ampersand
34. treble clef	B.	cent sign
35. 2/2 time	C.	greater-than sign
36. crescendo	D.	lower-case letter B
37. sharp	E.	pound sign

38. What seminal rock band's predecessor was known as Wicked Lester?

   a. Aerosmith
   b. Kiss
   c. Black Sabbath
   d. Journey

39. For what crime was Arlo Guthrie arrested, according to the lyrics of his Thanksgiving song favorite, "Alice's Restaurant"?

    a. fishing without a license
    b. speeding
    c. shoplifting
    d. littering

40. Spencer Eldon appeared wet and naked on the cover of what multi-platinum 1991 album?

41. What duo recorded songs for Vault and Reprise Records as Caesar and Cleo?

    a. Paul and Paula
    b. The Captain and Tennille
    c. Sonny and Cher
    d. Karen and Richard Carpenter

HITMAKING FORMULAE

These calculations are made with musical acts whose names end with a number (like, well, U2 and the Jackson 5, for instance). Place the correct numbers in the blanks and the calculations should work out mathematically.

A hint? Okay, here's a list of the numbers you'll use to fill in the blanks:

1, 3, 4, 5, 6, 6, 6, 7, 20, 40, and **42.**

(NEW COLONY x APOLLONIA) + FUN BOY + KRS = UB

(_____ x _____) + _____ + ____ = ____
   42.   43.   44.   45.   46.

VANITY	x	SYSTEM	=	LEVEL
_____	x	_____	=	_____
47.		48.		49.

GANG OF	x	THE COUNT	=	MATCHBOX
_____	x	_____	=	_____
50.		51.		52.

42. _____	46. _____	50. _____
43. _____	47. _____	51. _____
44. _____	48. _____	52. _____
45. _____	49. _____	

53. According to RIAA (Recording Industry Association of America) data from the last decade, about one in four musical recordings falls into this category, making it the most popular:

   a. rock
   b. country
   c. rap/hip-hop
   d. R&B

54. What is the top-selling double album in music history?

   a. *The Beatles (White Album)*, Beatles
   b. *The Wall*, Pink Floyd
   c. *Greatest Hits I and II*, Billy Joel
   d. *Frampton Comes Alive*, Peter Frampton

55. Which of the following was *NOT* one of the original inductees into the Rock 'n' Roll Hall of Fame?

    a. Bill Haley
    b. Elvis Presley
    c. Chuck Berry
    d. Fats Domino

56. NARAS, the organization that presents the Grammy Awards annually, is an abbreviation for National Academy of:

    a. Records, Albums and Singles
    b. Recording Arts and Sciences
    c. Radio, Audio and Sounds
    d. Record Auditing and Sales

57. True or False: Thomas Dolby, who enjoyed a hit with "She Blinded Me With Science," is an heir to the Dolby Sound Labs fortune.

REBEL REBEL

James Dean was a short-lived movie legend. He's been the subject of songs by everyone from Bonnie Tyler and the Eagles to Hillary Duff and the Goo Goo Dolls. His name has also appeared in the lyrics of several #1 pop hits, including these five. We'll provide the artist and the year, you name the song.

58. 1972, Don McLean: _____

59. 1982, John Mellencamp: _____

60. 1989, Michael Damian: _____

61. 1989, Billy Joel: _____

62. 1990, Madonna: _____

63. "The Alphabet Song" uses the same melody as what other popular children's song, published in 1806 by Jane Taylor?

64. What Grammy-winning musician is the son of the late Roxie Roker, who portrayed neighbor Helen Willis on TV's *The Jeffersons*?

JUST ADD SNAPPLE!

To answer the following question, place the seven letters that make up "SNAPPLE" in the correct blanks:

65. John McTammany revolutionized music in 1876 when he patented what keyboard instruments that could, amazingly, *play themselves*?

_ _ _ Y _ R   _ I A _ O _

66. *The New York Times* is mentioned in the lyrics of each of these 1970s songs, except:

    a. "Levon" by Elton John
    b. "New York State of Mind" by Billy Joel
    c. "Pop Muzik" by M
    d. "Stayin' Alive" by the Bee Gees

67. What is the real name of the rapper known variously as ODB, Dirt McGirt and Osirus?

68. Which of these successful male musicians did *NOT* grow up in and around the streets of Detroit?

    a. Eminem
    b. Mark McGrath
    c. Uncle Kracker
    d. Kid Rock

69. Tom Petty and the Heartbreakers hit it big with the album *Damn the Torpedoes,* an LP named after a famous quote by what celebrated U.S. admiral?

    a. James Farragut
    b. John Paul Jones
    c. William Halsey
    d. Chester Nimitz

AN "A" FOR EFFORT

In this quiz, the word(s) in each answer are special in that they contain no vowels *other than* A. You won't find an E, an I, an O, or a U in any of them. We even took out Y, just in case.

70. An early Rod Stewart single (with three words in its title): _____

71. This group hit #1 with a danceable version of "Venus": _____

72. Canadian singer of many hits, including "Angel" and "Adia": _____

73. Title track from the Steve Miller Band's 1982 album:_____

74. Band that previously brought fame to the father on TV's *The Osbournes*:_____

THE BLANK SONG

The six songs in this quiz are shown by their subtitles in Column A. Add one or more words in the blanks in Column B to complete the song's main title. In the example, "The Banana Boat Song" is also referred to by its subtitle, "Day-O."

COLUMN A	COLUMN B
EXAMPLE: "Day-O"	THE _BANANA BOAT_ SONG
75. "It's in His Kiss"	THE _____ SONG
76. "They Don't Write 'Em"	THE _____ SONG
77. "Christmas, Don't Be Late"	THE _____ SONG
78. "Feelin' Groovy"	THE _____ SONG
79. "Hey Hah"	THE _____ SONG
80. "There Is Love"	THE _____ SONG

AN IDOL THREAT

American Idol has been one of the decade's most successful TV shows. In the following quiz, combine the contestant's name with the title of his or her debut album. The example given is "WILLIAM HUNG – *INSPIRATION*." You'll place the other boxes the same way, with the artist first and then the album title. They'll only match one way.

The yellow boxes have already been placed in the clues to get you started.

A	CLARKSON	FANTASIA	KELLY
RUBEN	THANKFUL	AIKEN	CLAY
FREE	MAN	SKIES	WILLIAM
BARRINO	DeGARMO	HUNG	MEASURE
SOULFUL	YOURSELF	BLUE	DIANA
INSPIRATION	OF	STUDDARD	

EXAMPLE:	WILLIAM	HUNG	*INSPIRATION*

81. | | | | | *MAN* |

82.

83. | | | *FREE* | |

84.

85. | | | *THANKFUL* |

HEADLINE NEWS

The 1998 Grammy Awards ceremony was the scene of several rather bizarre events. Using the words "REAL" or "FAKE," verify the accuracy of these tabloid headlines that might have shown up in the week after the telecast.

86. *USHER INTRODUCES THE LEGENDARY BOB DYLAN AS "BILL"* _____

87. *ODB RUDELY INTERRUPTS SHAWN COLVIN'S ACCEPTANCE SPEECH* _____

88. *R. KELLY MAKES A SPLASH WEARING PRISON DENIMS* _____

89. *STING SNUBS EX-BANDMATES; REFUSES TO SHAKE HANDS* _____

90. *PAULA COLE MAKES RUDE HAND GESTURE WHILE SINGING* _____

MUSIC TELEVISION

Music videos have become an innovative art form. Following are five clues to the imagery in the music videos for the five songs below. Match the description to its corresponding video.

BACKWARDS CRASH   BEE GIRL   HAPPY DAYS

MOCKING MENTOS   DANCIN' WALKEN

91. BLIND MELON _____ "NO RAIN"

92. COLDPLAY _____ "THE SCIENTIST"

Sound off

93. FATBOY SLIM _____ "WEAPON OF CHOICE"

94. FOO FIGHTERS _____ "BIG ME"

95. WEEZER_____ "BUDDY HOLLY"

A BRAND NEW SHADE

With the assistance of the clues, name these "colorful" musical artists of the new millennium.

96. Known for dousing their audience with water guns:_____

97. Wrote and recorded a song with Justin Timberlake: _____

98. Toured with Snoop Dogg in 2003: _____

99. Won a 2000 Grammy for her single "I Try":

    _____

100. Supported the Rolling Stones on Fall 2005 tour dates: _____

1. (GI)RLSCH(OOL)

2. (MA)TCHST(ICK)

3. (O)FFSPR(ING)

4. **PRINCE**
   His birth name was
   Prince Rogers Nelson.

5. **B**
   The U.S. concert was held in
   Philadelphia.

6. **B**

7. **C**

8. **FALSE**
   "I'm a Little Teapot" was written by
   a pair of Tin Pan Alley songwriters
   in New York in 1939.

9. **SALT-N-PEPA**

10. **C**

11. **A**

12. **D**

13. **E**

14. **B**

15. **A**
    Schubert was a 19th-century
    composer who passed away in
    1828, shortly after his 30th
    birthday.

16. **THE BEATLES**
    The Beatles held all five positions,
    with (starting from #5, up)
    "Please Please Me," "I Want To
    Hold Your Hand," "She Loves You,"
    "Twist and Shout," and "Can't Buy
    Me Love."

17. **CHATTANOOGA,
    TENNESSEE**

18. **A**
    However, Andy had quite a solo
    career.

19. **B**

20. **C**
    Big Mountain's song was a cover
    of Peter Frampton's hit. Will to
    Power's "Baby I Love Your Way"
    was a different song that
    happened to have the same title.

21. **C**

22. **B**

23. **B**
    Paul Rodgers was formerly lead
    vocalist for Free and Bad
    Company. The tour was billed as
    Queen + Paul Rodgers.

24. **A**

25. **D**

26. **ROGER "SYD"
    BARRETT**
    Bassist Roger Waters, who took
    over the band after Syd's
    departure, goes by his middle
    name (his first name is George).

27. **A**

28. **"BURNING HEART"**
    The band also recorded "Eye of
    the Tiger," which was the theme
    from *Rocky III.*

29. **"CHARIOTS OF FIRE"**
    Evangelos is better known as Vangelis.

30. **JAMAICA**

31. **"GALVESTON," "WICHITA LINEMAN," "BY THE TIME I GET TO PHOENIX"**

32. **D**

33. **D**

34. **A**

35. **B**

36. **C**

37. **E**

38. **B**

39. **D**

40. *NEVERMIND* by **NIRVANA**
    Eldon was the baby in the pool on the album's front cover.

41. **C**

42. **6**

43. **6**

44. **3**

45. **1**

46. **40**

47. **6**

48. **7**

49. **42**

50. **4**

51. **5**

52. **20**

53. **A**
    While rock's popularity has dipped, it's still the most popular.

54. **B**
    By 1999, the album had sold 23 million copies, making it the third best-selling album (overall) in history.

55. **A**
    Of the choices, only Bill Haley wasn't part of the original 1986 class of inductees.

56. **B**

57. **FALSE**
    He was born Thomas Robertson, and became the subject of legal action after he found success using Dolby as his name.

58. **"AMERICAN PIE"**

59. **"JACK AND DIANE"**

60. **"ROCK ON"**

61. **"WE DIDN'T START THE FIRE"**

62. **"VOGUE"**

63. **"TWINKLE, TWINKLE, LITTLE STAR"**

64. **LENNY KRAVITZ**

65. **PLAYER PIANOS**

66. C

"Pop Muzik" mentions "New York" by name, but not its top-selling newspaper.

67. RUSSELL JONES

68. B

Mark McGrath was born in Hartford, Connecticut, and raised in California.

69. A

70. "HANDBAGS AND GLADRAGS"

71. BANANARAMA

72. SARAH McLACHLAN

73. "ABRACADABRA"

74. BLACK SABBATH

75. SHOOP SHOOP

76. BREAKUP

77. CHIPMUNK

78. 59th STREET BRIDGE

79. KETCHUP

80. WEDDING

81. CLAY AIKEN - *MEASURE OF A MAN*

82. DIANA DeGARMO - *BLUE SKIES*

83. FANTASIA BARRINO - *FREE YOURSELF*

84. RUBEN STUDDARD - *SOULFUL*

85. KELLY CLARKSON - *THANKFUL*

86. REAL

Dylan's appearance didn't get any less weird when a man with "SOY BOMB" painted on his chest began dancing next to him.

87. REAL

Colvin was accepting the Song of the Year award for "Sunny Came Home" when ODB grabbed the microphone and began rambling.

88. FAKE

89. FAKE

90. REAL

While performing "Where Have All the Cowboys Gone?," the camera had to quickly pan away from Paula Cole after she chose to give "the finger" during her act.

91. BEE GIRL

92. BACKWARDS CRASH

93. DANCIN' WALKEN

94. MOCKING MENTOS

95. HAPPY DAYS

96. GREEN DAY

97. BLACK-EYED PEAS

98. THE RED HOT CHILI PEPPERS

99. MACY GRAY

100. MAROON 5

Games
People Play

SPORTS & GAMES

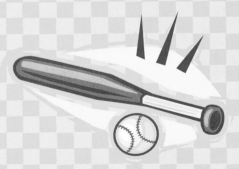

Face off, play ball, start your engines—whatever your sport of choice, there is a question in this GAMES PEOPLE PLAY section that will stump you. And for those confident readers who have their sports facts down cold, we've also included card game, board game, and computer game questions to even the playing field. Get ready to exercise your mind and see if you come close to par for the course.

BASEBALL

1. Hoyt Wilhelm was the first _____ pitcher to be elected to the Baseball Hall of Fame.

    a. left-handed
    b. relief
    c. Canadian-born
    d. knuckleball

2. The scorekeeper marks a strikeout with the letter K. What does it mean if the letter is written backwards?

    a. the count was full
    b. the batter did not swing at the third strike
    c. the catcher missed the ball
    d. the out ended the inning

3. What National League team beat the Chicago White Sox in the 1919 World Series, giving rise to the Black Sox scandal?

4. What American League team has used four different geographic designations without ever having left their home area?

5. In baseball, a 6-2 putout involves which of the following players?

   a. pitcher
   b. third baseman
   c. first baseman
   d. catcher

BASKETBALL

6. In men's college basketball, the games are _____ and the shot clock is _____ than in NBA games.

   a. longer, longer
   b. longer, shorter
   c. shorter, shorter
   d. shorter, longer

7. The team now known as the Washington Wizards began life under what name?

8. Until the 1930s, basketball rules called for what to occur after each field goal was scored?

   a. a free throw
   b. a jump ball
   c. a time out
   d. none of the above

9. The diameter of a regulation basketball is _____ that of a regulation basketball hoop.

   a. between one-quarter and two-fifths
   b. just less than half
   c. exactly half
   d. more than half

10. Unlike the NCAA college basketball tournament, the NIT (National Invitational Tournament) finals are played in the same arena each year. Name it.

FOOTBALL

11. In 1974, what team became the first in pro football to lose two Super Bowls?

    a. Minnesota Vikings
    b. Denver Broncos
    c. Dallas Cowboys
    d. Buffalo Bills

12. A football referee who makes a signal by placing both hands on his head is indicating:

    a. unsportsmanlike conduct
    b. personal foul
    c. ineligible player downfield
    d. illegal block

13. Through 2005, how many teams have won three consecutive Super Bowls?

14. How many members of the defense play "deep" (defending the pass) in what's known as a "dime" defense?

    a. 5
    b. 6
    c. 8
    d. 10

15. What city has hosted the Super Bowl eight times and played in the game five times, but never both at the same time?

ICE HOCKEY

16. Frederick Arthur is better known to the pro hockey world by what name?

17. What city's NHL team was the first to use artificial ice?

    a. Atlanta
    b. Toronto
    c. Los Angeles
    d. Boston

Name the NHL franchises that share their team names with:

18. an MLB team:_____

19. an NBA team:_____

20. an NFL team:_____

TEAM CINEMA

Name the pro sports team that employed the character in each of these films.

21. Edwina Franklin (Whoopi Goldberg) in *Eddie* (1996)

    a. New York Knicks
    b. Philadelphia 76ers
    c. Phoenix Suns
    d. Houston Rockets

22. Billy Chapel (Kevin Costner) in
    For Love of the Game (1999)

    a. Baltimore Orioles
    b. Cleveland Indians
    c. New York Yankees
    d. Detroit Tigers

23. Joe Pendleton (Warren Beatty) in
    Heaven Can Wait (1978)

    a. New York Giants
    b. Dallas Cowboys
    c. Houston Oilers
    d. Los Angeles Rams

24. Guffy McGovern (Paul Douglas) in
    Angels in the Outfield (1951)

    a. Washington Senators
    b. Los Angeles Angels
    c. Pittsburgh Pirates
    d. St. Louis Cardinals

25. Buck Weaver (John Cusack) in
    Eight Men Out (1988)

    a. Chicago White Sox
    b. Minnesota Twins
    c. Seattle Mariners
    d. Washington Senators

HARLEM GLOBETROTTERS

26. What 1958 member of the Harlem Globetrotters was the first team member whose jersey (#13) was retired?

    a. Oscar Robinson
    b. Wilt Chamberlain
    c. Nate Archibald
    d. Elvin Hayes

27. Known as the Harlem Globetrotters since 1930, the team originated three years earlier in what U.S. city?

    a. Philadelphia
    b. New York City
    c. Chicago
    d. Atlanta

28. What's the nickname of the Globetrotters' Michael Wilson, who in 2000 set a world record by dunking a basketball at a height of 12 feet (a full two feet above a standard rim)?

    a. the Orbit
    b. Wild Thing
    c. Air Man
    d. the Elevator

29. After the Washington Generals folded in 1995, what team stepped in as the new regular exhibition opponents of the Harlem Globetrotters?

    a. the Washington Stars
    b. the Brooklyn Bombers
    c. the Los Angeles Alarm
    d. the New York Nationals

30. In what comedy film did a referee in a Harlem Globetrotters game become possessed by one of the sons of Satan?

    a. *Bill and Ted's Bogus Journey*
    b. *Bedazzled*
    c. *Little Nicky*
    d. *Repossessed*

31. Which of these games begins with each player having the most pieces?

    a. checkers
    b. backgammon
    c. chess
    d. all above are the same

32. What toy item, invented in France, was first known as L'Ecran Magique?

    a. Etch-A-Sketch
    b. Magic 8-Ball
    c. Rubik's Cube
    d. Silly Putty

33. Which Monopoly railroad is absent from this list: Short Line, Reading, B&O.

34. What bonus is awarded in the middle square of Scrabble, given to the player who goes first?

    a. double letter score
    b. triple letter score
    c. double word score
    d. triple word score

35. When dealt a five-card stud hand of poker, odds are best that you'll end up with which of the following?

    a. one pair
    b. multiple cards of at least one suit
    c. no two cards of the same value
    d. at least one face card

36. How many feet wider is a doubles tennis court than a singles tennis court?

37. Who was the first "modern" heavyweight boxing champion (using Queensberry rules)?

    a. James J. Corbett
    b. John L. Sullivan
    c. Jack Dempsey
    d. James J. Jeffries

38. What sporting event was won by Clyde Van Dusen, Paul Jones, George Smith, and Joe Cotton?

    a. PGA Championship
    b. Indianapolis 500
    c. Kentucky Derby
    d. Wimbledon

39. True or False: The word "upset" came into use to mean a surprise outcome when a horse named Upset became the first to ever beat the legendary Man o' War.

40. What pro basketball star used his 6'10" frame and innovative hook shot to lead the Lakers to five championships?

CHESS

41. When playing chess, the Queen's bishop begins play in what position?

    a. second piece from the left
    b. third piece from the right
    c. third piece from the left
    d. depends on the color being played

42. What does the written notation "O-O" indicate in a chess game?

    a. a king-side castle
    b. a draw
    c. a zero-zero score
    d. checkmate

43. Who held the World Chess Championship title for more than a quarter of a century?

    a. Emanuel Lasker
    b. Boris Spassky
    c. Bobby Fischer
    d. Garry Kasparov

THE OLYMPIC GAMES

44. What city is scheduled to become the first to host the modern Olympic Games three times?

45. The modern Olympic Games began in Athens, Greece in 1896. In what year were women first allowed to participate?

46. Chosen by the IOC, what American city lost out on hosting the 1976 Winter Olympics when voters turned down the opportunity?

    a. Buffalo, New York
    b. Denver, Colorado
    c. Seattle, Washington
    d. Minneapolis, Minnesota

47. What Summer Olympic sport offers the widest variety of events?

    a. swimming
    b. gymnastics
    c. weightlifting
    d. track and field

48. In what year did the U.S. hockey team upset the U.S.S.R. in the gold medal game?

49. What was unique about marathon runner Abebe Bikila's gold medal for Ethiopia in the 1960 Summer Olympics?

    a. he ran barefoot
    b. he didn't finish the race
    c. he was 48 years old
    d. he wasn't from Ethiopia

50. Why is Zaire no longer represented at the Olympic Games?

    a. banned for continued drug use
    b. lack of Olympic funds
    c. participation banned by the government
    d. there is no longer any such nation

51. Through 2005, which of these countries has never had a Tour de France winner?

    a. U.K.
    b. Belgium
    c. Luxembourg
    d. France

52. Jim Roper won the very first NASCAR race, a 1949 event held at the Charlotte Speedway, driving what make of car?

    a. Hudson
    b. Lincoln
    c. Plymouth
    d. Studebaker

53. Which color of flag indicates that an auto race should come to a complete stop?

    a. red
    b. white
    c. black
    d. yellow

54. What swimming style provides the quickest race times?

    a. breaststroke
    b. freestyle
    c. butterfly
    d. backstroke

55. In 1999, who became the first undisputed heavyweight boxing champion in 12 years?

    a. Evander Holyfield
    b. Mike Tyson
    c. Michael Moorer
    d. Lennox Lewis

GAMES PEOPLE PLAY: SPORTS & GAMES

DOME SWEET DOME

It's not hard to fathom that the Georgia Dome is located in Atlanta or that the Alamodome is in San Antonio. Those with less descriptive names might be a bit more difficult, however. Identify the cities where these domed stadiums are located:

56. RCA Dome_____

57. Saddledome _____

58. Metrodome _____

STEVE Y.

Many pro sports stars have rather unusual names, and then there's good old "Steve Y." In pro baseball, football, and hockey, three men with this moniker won Championship MVPs in their respective leagues. You'll name them below.

Basketball doesn't fit into this equation. No "Steve Y" has won the NBA Finals MVP award. Catch up, guys!

59. PRO FOOTBALL: Steve Y_____ (Super Bowl MVP, 1995)

60. PRO BASEBALL: Steve Y_____ (World Series co-MVP, 1981)

61. PRO HOCKEY: Steve Y_____ (Stanley Cup MVP, 1998)

62. True or False: The Kentucky Derby is known as the "Run for the Roses," the Belmont is the "Run for the Carnations," and the Preakness is the "Run for the Black-Eyed Susans."

63. What woman did Bobby Riggs *defeat* in a celebrated 1973 tennis match?

64. In 1914 and again in 1915, Boston beat Philadelphia in baseball's World Series. Oddly, neither series pitted the same two teams against one another. Name all four teams that were involved in these two match-ups.

65. Which of these three-frame bowling sequences provides the highest potential third-frame score?

    a. X / 9-0
    b. / X 9-0
    c. 9-0 / X
    d. 9-0 X /

VOWEL OBSTRUCTION

Each of the three answers below contains five missing consonants. Place them in the blanks in the correct order and the answer to each clue will appear.

66. Ted Turner was a *Courageous* one of these sporting gents in 1974.

    Y A _ _ _ _ _ A N

67. Arms should be outstretched and 180° apart while participating in this sporting event.

    B A _ _ _ _ _ O K E

68. City that hosted the Winter Olympics in 1964 and 1976.

    I _ _ _ _ _ U C K

69. Place these four boxing weight divisions in order, from lightest to heaviest:

    BANTAMWEIGHT, FEATHERWEIGHT, FLYWEIGHT, LIGHTWEIGHT

70. Before Lance Armstrong, who was the only cyclist to win the Tour de France five consecutive years?

    a. Eddy Merckx
    b. Bernard Hinault
    c. Miguel Indurain
    d. Greg LeMond

71. The Ironman World Triathlon Championships are held annually in what exotic island location?

72. Name the only jockey to have guided two horses to the Triple Crown.

    a. Eddie Arcaro
    b. Steve Cauthen
    c. Willie Shoemaker
    d. Ron Turcotte

73. In 2002–03, which Williams sister defeated her sibling in all four Grand Slam women's tennis tournaments?

PUBLIC ADDRESS SYSTEM

See if you can identify these pro sports teams from their organization's street address.

EXAMPLE: 24 Willie Mays Plaza: <u>San Francisco Giants</u>

74. One Arrowhead Drive:_____

75. 1260 Rue de La Gauchetière:_____

76. 34 Kirby Puckett Place: _____

77. 2000 Gene Autry Way: _____

78. 755 Hank Aaron Drive: _____

79. Which M.J. has the second-highest number of career assists in NBA history?

    a. Michael Jordan
    b. Mark Jackson
    c. Magic Johnson
    d. none of the above

80. Since 1960, nearly all NFL season scoring leaders have been players at what position?

    a. running back
    b. wide receiver
    c. quarterback
    d. kicker

81. What popular game was invented in 1895 by the PE director of the YMCA in Massachusetts?

JUST ADD SNAPPLE!
To answer the following question, place the seven letters that make up "SNAPPLE" in the correct blanks:

82. What flashy pro wrestling move is a modified, dizzying version of the fireman's carry?

    _ I R _ _ A _ _   _ _ I N

83. Atlanta is home to four major league sports teams: the Braves, Falcons, Hawks, and Thrashers. Name the only pro team to move *from* Atlanta.

84. Which of the following earned golfer Jack Nicklaus his nickname, the Golden Bear?

    a. his high earnings
    b. his blonde hair
    c. his California home
    d. his high school's mascot

85. True or False: The Kentucky Derby has been run in Lexington every year since 1875.

86. How many different two-card combinations total 21 in the game of blackjack?

    a. 20
    b. 32
    c. 64
    d. 80

87. If you shuffle a deck of cards and deal yourself five every morning of the year, odds are that at least once before year's end, you'll deal yourself which of the following poker hands?

    a. flush
    b. full house
    c. four-of-a-kind
    d. straight

88. In the board game Mousetrap, what does the player do to initiate the contraption?

    a. turns a crank
    b. tips a bucket
    c. pushes a button
    d. drops a ball

89. What Bandai egg-shaped virtual pets were introduced to America in 1996?

90. In 1992, what became the first "new generation" first-person-shooter computer game, incorporating sound and better graphics?

    a. Quake
    b. Wolfenstein 3D
    c. Duke Nukem
    d. Doom

PICK-CUPS

Match the cup trophies in Column A to the sport in which the award is given from Column B.

COLUMN A	COLUMN B
91. America's Cup	A. Canadian Football
92. Davis Cup	B. Golf
93. Grey Cup	C. Soccer
94. Ryder Cup	D. Tennis
95. World Cup	E. Yachting

AN "A" FOR EFFORT

In this quiz, the word(s) in each answer are special in that they contain no vowels other than A. You won't find an E, an I, an O, or a U in any of them. We even took out Y, just in case.

96. This originally meant the part of a sports stadium covered by a roof: _____

97. This team from Texas played basketball in the old ABA: _____

98. In most forms of auto racing, this signal indicates that a driver should make an immediate pit stop:

_____

99. With 23 in his MLB career, Lou Gehrig hit more of these than anyone else: _____

100. What card game is known in many nations as vingt-et-un? _____

1. B

2. B
This is otherwise known as a "strikeout looking," because the batter simply watched the pitch instead of taking a hack at it.

3. CINCINNATI REDS
Beginning that year, the format was expanded from a best-of-seven to a best-of-nine, meaning the Reds had to win five games to take the Series.

4. ANGELS
Originally known as the L.A. Angels, they became the California Angels, then the Anaheim Angels, and are now known as the Anaheim Angels of Los Angeles.

5. D
In a 6-2 putout, the shortstop throws to the catcher.

6. D
In men's college basketball, the game is 30 minutes (vs. 36 in the pros) while the shot clock is 35 seconds (vs. 24).

7. CHICAGO PACKERS

8. B

9. D
A regulation hoop measures 18 inches, while a regulation basketball is 9.5 to 9.75 inches in diameter.

10. MADISON SQUARE GARDEN

11. A
Minnesota also lost the Super Bowl in 1970, 1975, and 1977. These four losses were by a combined score of 95-34.

12. C

13. NONE
The Packers, Dolphins, Steelers, 49ers, Cowboys, Broncos, and Patriots have won the championship back-to-back.

14. B
Add one defenseman to the traditional four to get five defenders, for a "nickel" defense. Add another "nickel" for a "dime" defense, and you'll have six defenders.

15. MIAMI
The city hosted the Super Bowl in 1968, '69, '71, '76, '79, '89, '95, and '99. The Dolphins played in the game in 1972, '73, '74, '83, and '85.

16. LORD STANLEY
He's the Stanley behind the NHL championship trophy, the Stanley Cup.

17. B
Frustrated with losing games to warm weather, the Toronto Arenas (now known as the Maple Leafs) first used "fake" ice in 1917.

18. RANGERS
The New York Rangers are the NHL team; the Texas Rangers play in MLB's American League.

19. KINGS
The Los Angeles Kings are the NHL team; the Sacramento Kings are in the NBA.

20. PANTHERS
The Florida Panthers are the NHL team; the Carolina Panthers are in the NFL.

21. A
Eddie also marked the feature film debut of New York City mayor Rudolph Giuliani.

22. D
It was Costner's third starring role in a baseball film, after *Bull Durham* and *Field of Dreams*.

23. D
The Rams moved to St. Louis before the start of the 1994 season.

24. C
The Los Angeles Angels began play in 1961.

25. A
The film told the story of the 1919 World Series.

26. B
After his one season with the Globetrotters, he joined the NBA's Philadelphia Warriors in 1959 and immediately won Rookie of the Year and League MVP honors.

27. C
The team was first known as the Savoy Big Five, but was renamed as a New York-based team to give the impression they were nationwide barnstormers.

28. B
"Wild Thing" was also the nickname of Rick Vaughn, the character portrayed by Charlie Sheen in the 1989 baseball comedy *Major League*.

29. D
The team is owned by Red Klotz, a former member of the Generals, who won only four games against the 'Trotters during his career.

30. C
In a cameo role, Dana Carvey portrayed this referee. *Little Nicky's* cast included several other *Saturday Night Live* alumni, including Jon Lovitz, Michael McKean, and Kevin Nealon.

31. CHESS
Chess begins with 16 pieces per side; backgammon, 15; checkers, 12.

32. A

33. PENNSYLVANIA
The real Short Line wasn't a railroad at all, but a bus service.

34. C

35. B
With any five cards, you're going to receive at least two of the same suit (since there are only four suits), so there's 100 percent chance of this occurring.

36. NINE FEET
When playing doubles, the lines are extended an additional 4.5 feet on each side of the court, adding nine feet to the width of the playing area.

37. A
James J. Corbett was heavyweight champ from 1892-1897.

38. C
They're not people; those were the names of horses who won the race.

39. TRUE
Upset beat Man o' War during the running of the Stanford Memorial on August 13, 1919.

40. GEORGE MIKAN
If you answered Kareem Abdul-Jabbar, don't feel bad. While Kareem did lead the L.A. Lakers to five titles and was known for his "sky hook," he was 7'2" tall. Mikan was 6'10", led the (then-Minneapolis) Lakers to five titles, and was a master of the "baby hook."

41. D
The Queen's bishop is on the left for the light-colored pieces, and on the right for the dark ones.

42. A

43. A

44. LONDON
The city hosted the Summer Games in 1908 and 1948, and was awarded the 2012 Games as well.

45. 1900

46. B
The 1976 Games were moved to Innsbruck, Austria.

47. D
As of the 2004 Games, there were 46 track and field events.

48. 1960
The 1980 "Miracle on Ice" game was better known, but it was a semi-final game and did not involve the gold medal.

49. A
He repeated as winner in 1964, but chose to wear shoes that time.

50. D
Zaire is now known as the Democratic Republic of the Congo.

51. A

52. B

53. A
A white flag indicates one lap left; a yellow flag means caution; a black flag indicates a forced pit stop.

54. B

55. D

56. INDIANAPOLIS

57. CALGARY

58. MINNEAPOLIS

59. STEVE YOUNG

60. STEVE YEAGER

61. STEVE YZERMAN

62. TRUE

63. MARGARET COURT
It was his defeat of the retired Court that inspired Riggs to arrange a second match later that year against Billie Jean King (who beat him). It was dubbed "The Battle of the Sexes."

64. ATHLETICS, BRAVES, PHILLIES, AND RED SOX
In 1914, the Boston Braves beat the Philadelphia Athletics. In 1915, the Boston Red Sox defeated the Philadelphia Phillies.

65. C
With a strike in the third frame, the potential highest score would be 59 (if it was followed by two more strikes)—higher than any of the other choices.

66. (YA)CHTSM(AN)

67. (BA)CKSTR(OKE)

68. (I)NNSBR(UCK)

69. FLYWEIGHT, BANTAMWEIGHT, FEATHERWEIGHT, LIGHTWEIGHT

70. C

71. HAWAII

72. A

73. SERENA
Serena beat Venus in the Australian Open, French Open, U.S. Open, and Wimbledon.

74. KANSAS CITY CHIEFS
The team plays their home games at Arrowhead Stadium.

75. MONTREAL CANADIENS

Since the Expos moved to Washington (and changed their name to the Washington Nationals), the Canadiens are the only major league sports team in that city.

76. MINNESOTA TWINS

Puckett wore #34 as a star for the team.

77. CALIFORNIA ANGELS OF LOS ANGELES

Gene Autry was formerly the team's owner. A statue of the country music star is located on the stadium grounds.

78. ATLANTA BRAVES

Hammerin' Hank hit 755 home runs, most of them in Milwaukee and Atlanta.

79. B

80. D

Kickers generally get more chances to score in games than any other player.

81. VOLLEYBALL

That's right; William Morgan of the Holyoke YMCA devised this game just four years after James Naismith came up with the idea of basketball at a different YMCA in nearby Springfield, Massachusetts.

82. AIRPLANE SPIN

83. THE FLAMES

Atlanta joined the NHL back in 1972; the team was sold and moved to Calgary, Alberta, Canada, in 1980. Surprisingly, the move was a financial decision by the owners and was not due to poor attendance.

84. D

Most attribute the nickname to his blonde hair and stocky build, but he garnered the name as a star athlete for the Golden Bears of Upper Arlington High in suburban Columbus, Ohio.

85. FALSE

While the event has been held every year since 1875, it takes place in Louisville, not Lexington.

86. C

The 10, J, Q, and K of each suit is worth 10, so there are 16 cards worth 10 points. Any of those 16 could be paired with any of the four aces to total 21. Thus, 16 x 4 = 64 possible combinations.

87. D

The odds of being dealt a straight are one in 255, so over a 365-day year, odds are that it will occur once.

88. A

In the game, the complicated device involves a boot kicking a bucket, a man diving into a barrel, and an unusual plumbing device.

89. TAMAGOTCHI

90. B

91. E

92. D

93. A

94. B

95. C

96. GRANDSTAND

97. DALLAS CHAPARRALS

98. BLACK FLAG

99. GRAND SLAMS

100. BLACKJACK

9

Wired & Moving

Technology &
Transportation

TECHNOLOGY AND TRANSPORTATION

It's time to speed things up! Log on and put the pedal to the metal and see how fast you can get through this road test in our **WIRED AND MOVING** section.

1. Which of the following forms of transportation was invented first?

   a. snowmobile
   b. submarine
   c. skateboard
   d. steam locomotive

2. Although his most famous discoveries were made after he emigrated to America, Alexander Graham Bell was born in:

   a. Canada
   b. China
   c. Germany
   d. Scotland

3. Philo Farnsworth and Vladimir Zworykin are widely co-credited with the invention of:

   a. the television
   b. fuel cells
   c. the portable defibrillator
   d. the microwave oven

4. True or False: Robert Bunsen invented the "burner" device that bears his name because his small laboratory required a portable source of flame.

5. Introduced in 1892, the Reno Inclined Elevator (later installed at Coney Island, NY) was considered the world's first practical:

   a. Ferris wheel
   b. escalator
   c. ski lift
   d. roller coaster

PERSONAL COMPUTERS

6. How much is a gigabyte?

   a. 1,024 megabytes
   b. 1,048,576 kilobytes
   c. 1,073,741,824 bytes
   d. all of the above

7. Which of the following was *not* a code added to Intel microchips to indicate they had extra processing power?

   a. TM
   b. DX2
   c. HT
   d. MMX

8. Which suffix is properly applied to the name of Microsoft co-founder Bill Gates?

   a. Jr.
   b. Sr.
   c. III
   d. none of the above

9. Which combination of names correctly lists the co-founders of Apple Computer?

   a. Steven Jobs and Steven Wozniak
   b. Stephen Jobs and Steven Wozniak
   c. Steven Jobs and Stephen Wozniak
   d. Stephen Jobs and Stephen Wozniak

10. Herman Hollerith's data processing machine was first successfully used in 1890 for tallying:

   a. presidential election votes
   b. census reports
   c. World's Fair attendance
   d. letters and packages

NERD ALERT!

Match the pair of computer innovators in Column A with their company in Column B.

EXAMPLE: Bill Gates and Paul Allen   MICROSOFT

COLUMN A	COLUMN B
11. Marc Andreessen and Jim Clarke	GOOGLE
12. Charles Geschke and John Warnock	YAHOO!
13. David Filo and Jerry Yang	eBAY
14. Sergey Brin and Larry Page	NETSCAPE
15. Pierre Omidyar and Jeff Skoll	ADOBE

16. True or False: To avoid confusion with toll-free 8XX numbers, no U.S. area codes begin with the number 8.

17. True or False: The price of Henry Ford's Model T car increased from $300 to $850 from 1908 to 1927.

18. On December 14, 1903, Wilbur Wright (and not his brother, Orville) got the opportunity to attempt the first manned, powered flight of a heavier-than-air craft because:

    a. it was his birthday
    b. 14 was his lucky number
    c. he was the older brother
    d. he won a coin toss

19. Why was a long spire constructed on top of New York's Empire State Building in 1931?

    a. to attract lightning
    b. to moor airships
    c. for daredevil circus acts
    d. to add world record height

JUST ADD SNAPPLE!
To answer the following question, place the seven letters that make up "SNAPPLE" in the correct blanks:

20. In 1948, George and Ladislao Biro patented what revolutionary instruments?

    B _ L _ _ O I _ T   _ _ N _

VOWEL OBSTRUCTION

Each of the three answers below contains five missing consonants. Place them in the blanks in the correct order and the answer to each clue will appear.

21. An anchored vessel used as a warning to watercraft.

    L I _ _ _ _ _ I P

22. Where you'd find a wiper on a British car.

    W I _ _ _ _ _ E E N

23. A "page description language" used by Adobe software.

    P O _ _ _ _ _ I P T

AN "A" FOR EFFORT

In this quiz, the word(s) in each answer are special in that they contain no vowels *other than* A. You won't find an E, an I, an O, or a U in any of them. We even took out Y, just in case.

24. This automotive part shares its name with a Tom Batiuk comic strip:_____

25. Named for the town where it set sail in 1819, this was the first steam-propelled ship to cross the Atlantic:_____

26. This construction and engineering marvel saved ships the long trip around the tip of South America:_____

27. Renault was the first automaker to build cars with this body style:_____

28. This California city is home to the high-tech capital, Silicon Valley:_____

29. *Geocaching* is a worldwide adventure game in which players use the Internet and what other electronic device?

30. Long-distance phone cards were first offered in what U.S. state (known for its notoriously high calling rates)?

    a. California
    b. New Jersey
    c. Florida
    d. Hawaii

31. What is the popular term used to refer to a surprise feature or bonus hidden inside an electronic medium?

32. If it were in a straight line, the total distance of the track on a typical compact disc would be how long?

    a. 18 inches
    b. 370 feet
    c. 3 miles
    d. 4,500 km

33. Which side of a phonograph record's groove provides the left-channel stereo output, the inner edge or the outer edge?

34. Which of the following Boeing airliners has the largest passenger capacity?

    707, 717, 727, 737, 747, 757, 767, or 777?

35. Which of these flights from Washington, D.C., travels the longest distance?

    a. Seattle
    b. London
    c. Los Angeles
    d. Mexico City

36. Which of the following binary numbers is equivalent to the year Christopher Columbus "discovered" America?

    a. 11101011110
    b. 10111010100
    c. 11111010001
    d. 11010000010

37. True or False: While now known for electronics, the first item sold under the Sharp brand name was a mechanical pencil.

SST? MIA!

The Concorde supersonic transport no longer makes flights, but it was *the* elite way to travel for several years. See how much you remember about this unique plane that could fly twice the speed of sound.

38. True or False: The one and only crash involving the Concorde was the result of a flat tire.

39. A total of 14 Concordes were used in regular air service; seven owned by _____ and seven owned by _____.

    a. KLM, Delta Airlines
    b. Swiss Air, United Airlines
    c. Air France, British Airways
    d. Virgin Atlantic, TWA

40. What British musician flew on the Concorde so he could perform at both the London and Philadelphia portions of 1985's Live Aid concert?

    a. Sting
    b. Paul McCartney
    c. Phil Collins
    d. David Bowie

AW, SHOOT

Technology has taken us from the slingshot to the atomic bomb, but we'll admit it: Our favorite guns are the ones that *don't* fire anything lethal.

41. The world's oldest and largest manufacturer of BB guns is known by what flowery name?

    a. Lily
    b. Daisy
    c. Carnation
    d. Rose

42. Often seen in comic book advertisements of the past, a special gun could fire "harmless pellets" a distance of up to 50 feet using what vegetable?

    a. lima beans
    b. carrots
    c. pumpkins
    d. potatoes

43. In Disney's animated 1946 adaptation of *Peter and the Wolf*, young Peter attempts to capture the wolf using what type of weapon?

    a. pop gun
    b. water gun
    c. dart gun
    d. pellet gun

44. The live-action game sometimes known as Pursuit uses what type of ammunition?

    a. foam darts
    b. paintballs
    c. electronic beams
    d. rubber bullets

45. True or False: While being a member of AA may raise your car insurance rates in the United States, it may lower them in the United Kingdom.

46. What beneficial feature wasn't added to the wheel until some 1,500 years after its invention by the Sumerians in about 3500 B.C.?

    a. axle
    b. spokes
    c. hub
    d. tire

47. While performing early experiments with the light bulb, which of the following did Thomas Edison find could be used in filaments that lasted up to 900 hours?

   a. copper
   b. tungsten
   c. bamboo
   d. platinum

48. Which of the following temperature scale namesakes also invented the mercury thermometer?

   a. Kelvin
   b. Fahrenheit
   c. Celsius
   d. none of the above

49. What automotive company was the first to install three-point safety belts in its vehicles as standard equipment?

   a. Volvo
   b. Vauxhall
   c. Volkswagen
   d. Volga

50. To take advantage of its cute, face-like front end, the Dodge/Plymouth Neon was introduced to the world in advertisements featuring a head-on photo and what one-word greeting?

   a. "Hi."
   b. "Yo."
   c. "Howdy."
   d. "Aloha."

ROAD SIGNS

You can tell a lot about a road sign by its shape and color. Here are seven phrases you might see on road signs along an Interstate highway. You match the color from the list below to the correct sign.

BLUE **BROWN** **GREEN** **ORANGE**
RED **WHITE** **YELLOW**

SIGN TEXT	COLOR
51. WRONG WAY	_____
52. ROAD CONSTRUCTION AHEAD	_____
53. NATIONAL PARK	_____
54. EXIT 93-B	_____
55. SPEED ZONE AHEAD	_____
56. SLIPPERY WHEN WET	_____
57. REST AREA	_____

58. "We have the technology…" intoned the voice at the beginning of what television series?

    a. *Quantum Leap*
    b. *The Six Million Dollar Man*
    c. *Sliders*
    d. *Battlestar: Galactica*

59. What technology was first used on the long-forgotten TV program *The Hank McCune Show*?

    a. color images
    b. stereo sound
    c. canned laughter
    d. tape delay

60. The names of which two of Santa's reindeer were also used as the names of cars built by Mercury and Volkswagen, respectively?

TRAVELING BAND

Musical acts usually do quite a bit of traveling to showcase their abilities to as many of their fans as possible via live concerts. Fill in the correct words to complete the titles of these hit "traveling" songs:

EXAMPLE: "___LAST___ ___TRAIN___ TO_LONDON_"
by the Electric Light Orchestra

---

61. "_____ _____ TO _____"
    by Talking Heads

62. "_____ _____ TO _____"
    by Gladys Knight and the Pips

63. "_____ _____ TO _____"
    by the Monkees

64. "_____ _____ TO _____"
    by The Rose Garden

65. "_____ _____ TO _____"
    by Eddie Money

BR-549

If you drive a Corvette or a Pinto, people know what your car is like. But behind the wheel of a 300M or an F250, it's all about the numbers. This quiz concerns automobiles that are better known by number and/or letter sequences.

66. What Japanese automaker produced the 110, 210, 310, 410, 510, 610, 710, 810, and (wait for it) 910 models?_____

67. What American automaker offered the 1000, 2000, and 6000, and also spiced things up by making the T1000 and (gasp) the J2000?

_____

68. L7... M3... X5... Z8... bingo! What European carmaker's models include these (and several other) alpha-numerically named autos?

_____

TECH VS. TEXT

In this short quiz, we'll examine the relationship between the science of technology and the art of fiction.

69. Using logic more than literary license, how many laws did Isaac Asimov and John Campbell feel were necessary for a human-like robot to safely function (as depicted in the story *I, Robot*)?

70. True or False: Author William S. Burroughs, whose novels included *Naked Lunch*, was the son of the inventor of the first adding machine.

71. William Gibson coined what tech-happy word in his 1984 novel, *Neuromancer*?

    a. automaton
    b. software
    c. cyberspace
    d. hypertext

72. True or False: The first subway built in North America was constructed underneath Tremont Avenue in New York City.

73. Which number is the name of both the first Atari video game console and a quarterly magazine dedicated to computer hackers?

    a. 256
    b. 714
    c. 1038
    d. 2600

74. What online service best completes this analogy?

    SEARS was to PRODIGY as H&R BLOCK was to

    _____.

75. What aspect of the computer gave the Commodore 64 its numeric name?

    a. 64 kilobytes of memory
    b. 64 MHz processor
    c. $64 suggested retail price
    d. all of the above

TECH TIMELINE

In each set of two choices, which computer/online innovation was introduced to the public *first?*

76. GOOGLE / YAHOO!

77. AMERICA ONLINE / THE WORLD WIDE WEB

78. CD-ROM DRIVE / THE PENTIUM CHIP

79. True or False: The Hewlett-Packard computer company was organized from the former PC sales leader, Packard-Bell.

80. Completed in 1977, the Alaska Pipeline carries oil along what path?

   a. from Alaska to Washington
   b. from northern Alaska to southern Alaska
   c. from Alaska to Canada
   d. from Canada to Alaska

81. True or False: The British government has a greater than 50 percent stake in British Petroleum.

82. What does the V stand for in the V-chip, the device used to select appropriate television programming for children?

   a. video
   b. viewer
   c. violence
   d. voluntary

83. What two-letter suffix has *not* been used to indicate a variety of Microsoft Windows operating system software?

    a. XP
    b. AV
    c. CE
    d. NT

84. What nickname is most commonly used by Brits to refer to the BBC (British Broadcasting Corporation) network?

    a. Bobby
    b. Beecee
    c. Beeb
    d. Beback

STATION TO STATION

A transportation test wouldn't be complete without a quiz concerning trains.

85. The Orient Express whisked travelers from _____ to _____ (and back again).

    a. France, Turkey
    b. Greece, China
    c. Spain, India
    d. Portugal, Mongolia

86. What brightly colored train traveled along the Rock Island Line?

    a. Orange Blossom Special
    b. Rocket
    c. Fireball
    d. Wabash Cannonball

87. True or False: Later the subject of a popular ballad, Casey Jones was a real-life engineer aboard the Cannonball Express for the Illinois Central Railroad.

88. In the early 20th century, the Santa Fe Railroad's luxury Chief, Super Chief, and El Capitán trains linked what Midwestern city with Los Angeles?

    a. Detroit
    b. Cleveland
    c. Chicago
    d. St. Louis

CAR-AZY

Following are groups of cars of the past or present whose names begin with the letter C. Three cars in each group were made by the same automaker, the fourth was not. Identify the "odd vehicle out" in each group.

EXAMPLE:
CHARGER, CIVIC, CARAVAN, CHALLENGER:
<u>CIVIC</u>_____ *(Dodge makes all of these except the Civic)*

---

89. CAVALIER, CORSICA, CELEBRITY, CAPRI:

   _____

90. CONCORDE, CORONA, CORDOBA, CIRRUS:

   _____

91. CATERA, CRESSIDA, CELICA, CAMRY:

   _____

92. CORTINA, CONTOUR, CITATION, CROWN VICTORIA

   _____

93. CORRADO, COMMANDO, CJ-7, CHEROKEE

   _____

94. True or False: Early hackers found a way to trigger free telephone service using the pitch made by a whistle found in boxes of Cap'n Crunch cereal.

95. How did the first man in space, Yuri Gagarin, return to Earth?

    a. His craft landed in the Pacific.
    b. He was ejected and parachuted to Earth.
    c. His craft was parachuted to Earth.
    d. none of the above

96. True or False: The U.S. government contracted for development of a "stink" chemical, called Who Me?, to be sprayed on German troops during World War II.

97. What e-mail service has more than 170 million active users worldwide, making it the largest in existence?

    a. Yahoo!
    b. Hotmail
    c. America Online
    d. MSN

98. While they never landed on the moon as planned, the crewmembers of Apollo 13 do hold which of the following records?

    a. the humans farthest from Earth
    b. the longest Apollo journey
    c. the first images of the far side of the Moon
    d. the first NASA astronauts killed in space

99. In 1990, advances in archaeological techniques helped researchers locate the largest *T. rex* skeleton ever discovered, found in:

    a. Ethiopia
    b. Paraguay
    c. Siberia
    d. South Dakota

100. Datsun-Nissan's legendary series of Z cars began with what effeminate name?

    a. Fairlady
    b. Rose
    c. Damsel
    d. Queen

1. **B**
   The first submarine, the Turtle, was used by the colonists during the American Revolution.

2. **D**

3. **A**

4. **FALSE**
   Although Bunsen popularized the burner, it was Michael Faraday who invented the device.

5. **B**

6. **D**

7. **A**

8. **C**
   His full name is William Henry Gates, III.

9. **C**

10. **B**

11. **NETSCAPE**

12. **ADOBE**

13. **YAHOO!**

14. **GOOGLE**

15. **eBAY**

16. **FALSE**
    The only numbers that are restricted from being the first number in an area code are 0 and 1.

17. **FALSE**
    In fact, it's the other way around. The price dropped from $850 to $300, thanks to better production techniques and improved technology.

18. **D**
    Sadly, he damaged the craft in a crash just after takeoff, and it was brother Orville who finally took to the air three days later.

19. **B**
    Due to high winds at that altitude, however, no dirigible ever attempted to approach the building.

20. **BALLPOINT PENS**

21. **(LI)GHTSH(IP)**

22. **(WI)NDSCR(EEN)**

23. **(PO)STSCR(IPT)**

24. **CRANKSHAFT**

25. **SAVANNAH**

26. **PANAMA CANAL**

27. **HATCHBACK**

28. **SANTA CLARA**

29. **GPS**
    (GLOBAL POSITIONING SYSTEM)

30. **D**

31. **EASTER EGG**

32. **C**

33. **THE INNER EDGE**

34. **747**
    The 747 still accommodates more passengers than any other airliner in the series: between 490 and 630, depending on the configuration.

35. **B**
    The distance from Washington to London is more than 3,500 miles, over 1,000 miles more than any other trip in the choices.

36. **C**

37. **TRUE**

38. **TRUE**

39. **C**

40. C

41. B

42. D

43. A

44. B

45. TRUE
In the U.S., AA stands for Alcoholics Anonymous. In the U.K., it's the Automobile Association (the equivalent of the AAA in the U.S.).

46. B
Spokes allowed for a lighter wheel, an improvement that greatly enhanced the development of wheeled vehicles.

47. C
Tungsten filaments are commonly used in the light bulbs of today.

48. B

49. A

50. A

51. RED

52. ORANGE

53. BROWN

54. GREEN

55. WHITE

56. YELLOW

57. BLUE

58. B

59. C

60. COMET, DASHER

61. THE ROAD to NOWHERE

62. MIDNIGHT TRAIN to GEORGIA

63. LAST TRAIN to CLARKSVILLE

64. NEXT PLANE to LONDON

65. TWO TICKETS to PARADISE

66. DATSUN/NISSAN

67. PONTIAC

68. BMW

69. THREE
The three laws were: (First Law) A robot may not injure a human being, or, through inaction, allow a human being to come to harm. (Second Law) A robot must obey the orders given it by human beings except where such orders would conflict with the First Law. (Third Law) A robot must protect its own existence as long as such protection does not conflict with the First or Second Law.

70. FALSE
The author was the inventor's grandson.

71. C

72. FALSE
North America's first subway was built in Boston.

73. D

74. COMPUSERVE
Just as Sears began the Prodigy service, H&R Block was the initial driving force behind CompuServe.

75. A

76. YAHOO!
Yahoo! began in 1985; Google a year later.

77. AMERICA ONLINE
America Online (renamed from earlier incarnations) began in 1989; the WWW premiered in 1991.

78. CD-ROM DRIVE
Intel's first Pentium chip came about four years after the 1989 introduction of the CD-ROM drive.

79. FALSE
The companies existed concurrently and were unrelated. Packard-Bell merged with NEC in 1996 and soon closed its U.S. offices.

80. B
The pipeline takes oil from Prudhoe Bay in northern Alaska to the port city of Valdez in southern Alaska.

81. FALSE
The British government held a controlling (51%) interest in BP at the end of World War I. The government stake in the company was sold gradually over a 10-year period and was gone by 1995.

82. B

83. B

84. C

85. A
The train traveled between Paris, France, and Constantinople (now Istanbul), Turkey.

86. B

87. TRUE

88. C

89. CAPRI
(Mercury, others are Chevy)

90. CORONA
(Toyota, others are Chrysler)

91. CATERA
(Cadillac, others are Toyota)

92. CITATION
(Chevy, others are Ford)

93. CORRADO
(VW, others are Jeep)

94. TRUE
Savvy tech types discovered that the toy whistle (a premium in Cap'n Crunch cereal boxes) emitted a tone which, when sounded into a telephone receiver, tripped the long distance trunking mechanism, opening the way for free phone calls.

95. B
Gagarin's craft, the Vostok I, ejected him after it had re-entered the Earth's atmosphere, and he parachuted safely to the ground. It was many years before the USSR attempted the "splashdown" landings used by NASA.

96. TRUE
The foul-smelling chemical was said to put off a strong odor resembling rotting garbage.

97. B

98. A
Their wide turn around the moon took them nearly 250,000 miles away from Earth, farther than any other human has been before or since.

99. D

100. A

10

Snapple
Blends

A POTPOURRI OF
MISCELLANEOUS TRIVIA

What can you say about a grab bag of questions? It's simple:
Our SNAPPLE BLENDS section contains clever and snappy
questions that didn't fit anywhere else. Call it a hodgepodge,
a jumble, or potpourri, but dig in and have fun!

1. Which Zodiac sign is *NOT*
   represented by a human or
   animal creature?

2. What color swimsuit did Farrah Fawcett wear in
   the photograph depicted in her best-selling 1976
   poster?

   a. red
   b. blue
   c. black
   d. white

3. Any month containing a Friday the 13th begins
   on what day of the week?

4. What objects are collected by *aerophilatelists?*

   a. Frisbees
   b. UFO photos
   c. air mail stamps
   d. air sickness bags

5. What IZOD creature appeared on the left chest of
   nearly all 1980s preppies?

MOVIE-MOTIVATED FADS

Throughout Hollywood's history, theater-goers have emulated their big-screen heroes in many ways. Some of the biggest trends in the 1970s and 80s were inspired by motion pictures. Name the movies that spawned the following fads. The films' release years are provided as hints:

6. Women wearing oversized men's clothes (1977):
   _____

7. Toga parties (1978): _____

8. Mechanical bulls in bars (1980): _____

9. Ray-Ban sunglasses (1980): _____

10. Torn sweatshirts and pants (1983): _____

11. "Madison" as a girls' name (1985): _____

RUBBERY WRISTS

Below is a sentence about the "cause bracelet" fad that's grown steadily over the past few years. Fill in the three blanks with the proper answers.

Yellow rubber bracelets supporting___#12___ research, were inspired by___#13___and were inscribed with the two-word motto,___#14___.

12. _____

13. _____

14. _____

Snapple Blends

NO KID-DING!

Celebrities have outdone themselves in recent years by finding odd names for their offspring. Here, you'll match up the star mother or father in *Column A* with the child's name in *Column B*.

COLUMN A	COLUMN B
EXAMPLE: BONO ——————→ (lead singer for U2)	GUGGI Q
15. NICOLAS CAGE (*Leaving Las Vegas* Oscar winner)	APPLE
16. PENN GILLETTE (of the comedy team Penn & Teller)	BANJO
17. RACHEL GRIFFITHS (star of *Six Feet Under*)	KAL-EL
18. JASON LEE (star of *My Name Is Earl*)	MOXIE
19. GWYNETH PALTROW (star of *Shakespeare in Love*)	PILOT

20. Chocolate chip cookies were invented in which century?

   a. the 9th
   b. the 13th
   c. the 17th
   d. the 20th

21. What English word appears on all regular-issue U.S. coins, but not on our nation's paper money?

22. The social phenomenon that occurs when groups of people phone and message one another to meet *en masse* in a public place is known as:

23. Getting old isn't fun, but it's better than the alternative. It's also the only way to gain membership into AARP, for which you must reach the age of:

    a. 40
    b. 50
    c. 55
    d. 60

24. The Bermuda Triangle (or Devil's Triangle), where several ships and planes have been said to vanish mysteriously, is defined as the area between Bermuda, the southern tip of Florida, and:

    a. Puerto Rico
    b. Cuba
    c. Brazil
    d. Cancun, Mexico

25. True or False: Japanese golfers take out insurance policies against scoring an ace while golfing, which only pay if they manage to achieve a hole-in-one.

FUZZY LOGIC

Sometimes, creatures made out to be "cute" end up being merely annoying. Had these three examples become as popular as their developers hoped, secondhand shops nationwide would be filled with little stuffed dolls representing them. Luckily, we were spared.

26. A sinister, brown, fuzzy (and rather nondescript) puppet character named Bad Andy spent a few months wreaking havoc at which restaurant chain?

    a. Wendy's
    b. Domino's
    c. Taco Bell
    d. McDonald's

27. What furry blue mascot didn't perform its intended duty of putting a happy face on the 1996 Summer Olympic Games in Atlanta?

    a. Lanty
    b. Olly
    c. Izzy
    d. Sporty

28. Many fans rolled their eyes at what "kid-friendly" *Episode I: The Phantom Menace* character, and cheered when his speaking role was greatly reduced in the final two installments of *Star Wars?*

    a. Wicket
    b. Jabba the Hut
    c. Yoda
    d. Jar Jar Binks

FAD DOG!

It's difficult to admit that living creatures have sometimes been reduced to fad status, but anyone who shelled out $1.25 for sea monkeys, expecting them to put on a nightly circus show, understands the truth. Here are some gotta-have-'em canines of the past 50 years.

29. The hit TV series *Frasier* and successful film *My Dog Skip* coerced many to run out and purchase what breed of dog? _____

30. A 1996 film led to the increased popularity of what breed, despite warnings that they were aggressive, hyperactive, and often suffered from hearing disorders?_____

31. In the 1980s, Spuds McKenzie was all the rage, but in the 1990s, the advertising canine of note was Gidget, a talking _____

32. Many Americans still called them Alsatians in the 1950s, when what type of dog became the top-registered AKC breed of the decade? _____

33. True or False: One of the more popular "fad" dogs of recent note is the Labradoodle, a cross between a Labrador Retriever and a Poodle. _____

A TEST TEST

Throughout life, we have to take all kinds of tests. Driving tests, stress tests, maybe even *The Snapple Aptitude Test*. Here, for the first time, is a test about tests to test your test-taking ability.

Use the tests in the following list to correctly fill in the five blanks below:

ABO TEST
FRIEDMAN TEST
RORSCHACH TEST
SNELLEN TEST
TURING TEST

34. If you see blotches before your eyes, you're probably taking this test. _____

35. You might get an A+ on this test, or you might get a B-. _____

36. This test is usually taken from a distance of 20 feet away. _____

37. One creature in particular is hoppin' happy that this test is no longer used. _____

38. You'd have to be a machine to take this kind of test. _____

TEA FOR THREE

Snapple knows tea, so you should know T. Identify these two-word titles that begin with T, end with T, and have T in the middle. Use the entries in the filler list to fill in the blanks.

FILLER LIST:

AKE	~~OR~~
HA	RIO
HE	RO
HEPA	URKEY
HNIGH	WELF
~~ILLAFLA~~	WIS

EXAMPLE: T _OR_ T _ILLAFLA_ T   a novel (1930s)

---

39. T _____ T _____ T   a play (1600s)

40. T _____ T _____ T   a dance (1890s)

41. T _____ T _____ T   a song and dance (1950s)

42. T _____ T _____ T   a vocal group (1990s)

43. T _____ T _____ T   a movie (2000s)

EPONYM T AND F

Eponyms are items that share their name with the person who invented, discovered, or otherwise made them popular. Diesel fuel, for instance, was developed by Rudolf Diesel. These five... well, they might not prove quite so easy.

44. True or False: The saxophone was named after Antoine J. Sax.

45. True or False: It may sound fishy, but the fish species known as the guppy was named after an English scientist named Robert Guppy.

46. True or False: A British army officer named Henry Shrapnel invented an artillery shell whose fragments became commonly known as shrapnel.

47. True or False: The Rockola jukebox is named after its inventor, David Rockola.

48. True or False: George Eastman named Kodak after a Native American guide who accompanied him on a photography trip to the American southwest.

VOWEL OBSTRUCTION

Each of the three answers below contains five missing consonants. Place them in the blanks in the correct order and the answer to each clue will appear.

49. Boys who recorded the albums *Black and Blue* and *Never Gone*.

    B A _ _ _ _ _ E E T

50. Bob who wrote, directed, and starred in the 1992 film *Shakes the Clown*.

    G O _ _ _ _ _ A I T

51. A kids' game alternately known as spillikins or pick-up sticks.

    J A _ _ _ _ _ A W S

AN "A" FOR EFFORT

In this quiz, the word(s) in each answer are special in that they contain no vowels *other than* A. You won't find an E, an I, an O, or a U in any of them. We even took out Y, just in case.

52. This cream-and-milk combination is good in coffee or hot tea: _____

53. The four-word finish to the lyric: "C'mon, babe, why don't we paint the town?"

    _____

54. This was the title of Van Halen's last hit with David Lee Roth before they parted ways.

    _____

55. Lorne Greene, Hank Aaron, and Mickey Mouse have held this Rose Bowl Parade position.

    _____

56. "Laughter is contagious" was the tagline for what 1998 Robin Williams film? _____

LIQUID REFRESHMENT

Okay, you've worked hard on the test thus far, and it's time for a drink. If you're out of Snapple Lemonade, we'll have to substitute some other kind of "-ade" to quench your thirst. Use the clues to place the correct term (all end with "-ade") in the blanks provided.

EXAMPLE:

A DEVICE TO BLOCK SOLAR RAYS: <u>SUNSHADE</u>

57. A STYX SONG OR JEEP VEHICLE: _____

58. THE CAPITAL OF SERBIA: _____

59. A JAIL ON A MILITARY BASE: _____

60. A ROMANTIC MUSICAL COMPOSITION: _____

61. A SWEET, JELLY-LIKE FRUIT SPREAD: _____

EVERYONE KNOWS IT'S WENDY

Wendy the Snapple Lady is just one of many famous Wendys to have graced the world with her presence.

62. What's the last name of Wendy and her siblings in *Peter Pan?*

63. *Wendy the Good Little Witch* has appeared in scores of cartoons and comic books for what entertainment company?

64. What charitable cause hit home with Dave Thomas, founder of Wendy's restaurants, because it had affected him personally as a child?

65. What two-word greeting did Jack Torrance (Jack Nicholson) famously scream to his wife Wendy (Shelley Duvall) while hacking his way through a door with an axe in the 1980 horror film *The Shining*?

66. Playwright Wendy Wasserstein won a 1989 Tony and a Pulitzer Prize for what popular play?

MUST-HAVE TOYS

If you were a kid, you had them. If you were a parent, you bought them.

Following are four characters (or sets of characters) that were some of the most popular toys of their time. Place them in the order of their *first* appearance on store shelves, from oldest to newest.

CABBAGE PATCH KIDS

MY LITTLE PONY

STRAWBERRY SHORTCAKE

TICKLE-ME ELMO

67. _____

68. _____

69. _____

70. _____

Had enough? No? Here are four more characters (or sets of characters) that were also some of the must-have toys of their time. Place them in the order of their *first* appearance on store shelves, from oldest to newest.

CARE BEARS
FURBY
TEDDY RUXPIN
POUND PUPPIES

71. _____

72. _____

73. _____

74. _____

DO THE (NEW) WAVE

New Wave music wasn't just about music; it was about image, or sometimes even a gimmick. Here's a quick ABC (okay, it's an ABCDE) of New Wave bands and artists. The first starts with A, the second with B, and so on. The clues will guide you along.

75. Band dressed as pirates with war paint and used *two* drummers:

A _____

76. Female members of this band sported exaggerated beehive hairdos:

B _____

77. The androgynous lead
    singer had long braids,
    an oversized white tunic,
    and *lots* of eye makeup:

    C _____

78. Band members variously
    wore yellow boiler suits or
    red flower pots:

    D _____

79. Singer/guitarist known
    for his oversized,
    Buddy Holly-style glasses:

    E _____

I'VE SEEN THIS BEFORE

A trend that's extended well into the 2000s is Hollywood's desire to redo and revamp hit films of the past. With this in mind, test your analogy skills in the following six sequences about actors appearing in movies that have been remade in the last few years.

80. In the film *The Bad News Bears*:
    WALTER MATTHAU is to _____
    as TATUM O'NEAL is to SAMMI KANE KRAFT.

81. In the film *The Stepford Wives*:
    _____ is to NICOLE KIDMAN
    as PAULA PRENTISS is to BETTE MIDLER.

82. In the film *Alfie*:
    SHELLEY WINTERS is to MARISA TOMEI
    as MICHAEL CAINE is to _____.

83. In the film *Freaky Friday:*
BARBARA HARRIS is to JAMIE LEE CURTIS
as JODIE FOSTER is to _____.

84. In the film *The Alamo:*
_____ is to BILLY BOB
THORNTON
as RICHARD WIDMARK is to JASON PATRIC.

85. In the film *The Longest Yard:*
BURT REYNOLDS is to ADAM SANDLER
as JAMES HAMPTON is to _____.

86. Cornelius McGillicuddy was:

   a. Lucille Ball's father
   b. a pro baseball player
   c. inventor of the chainsaw
   d. all of the above

87. The "lemniscate" is the proper name for what
symbol?

   a. the pound sign
   b. the infinity sign
   c. the asterisk
   d. the "at" sign

88. The 1974 motion picture *Stay Hungry*
documented which of the following?

   a. bodybuilding
   b. pie-eating contests
   c. rock music
   d. inner city gangs

FEEL LIKE A NUMBER?

Numbers play an important part in baseball. Luckily, even if you don't know sports, your knowledge in other fields may help you with this particular quiz.

Column A contains a list of baseball clues that all have numbers as their answer. Column B contains other sources that reference the same number. You place the correct matching number in the blank between the two columns.

EXAMPLE:

| Number of players in the field for the defense | 9 | Number of states needed to ratify the original U.S. Constitution |

COLUMN A		**COLUMN B**
89. Babe Ruth's career HR total	_____	Badge number of *Dragnet's* Joe Friday
90. Minimum distance traveled (in feet) to circle the bases	_____	Number of degrees in a circle
91. Jersey number worn by Hank Aaron	_____	Year B.C. in which Julius Caesar was assassinated
92. Width of home plate (in inches)	_____	Title of a hit single by rock group Winger
93. Number of double stitches on a Major League baseball	_____	Solution of the calculation $1^1 \times 2^2 \times 3^3 = ?$

A SPELL ON YOU

So you're a good speller? No trouble with *pneumonia* or *ukulele?* Great! Let's see how you are at correctly spelling these celebrity names (first and last).

94. He's the Canadian comic who starred in a variety of films, from *Nothing but Trouble* to *My Girl*.

   _____

95. She bombed as Molloy Martin in the 1990 TV series *Molloy*, but hit it big a year later as Blossom Russo in *Blossom*.

   _____

96. This actor was *Charmed* to be a part of a new hit TV series after the inconsistencies that resulted in her removal from *Beverly Hills, 90210*.

   _____

97. Born and raised in Atlanta, this actor was best known for his portrayal of Leonard McCoy on *Star Trek*.

   _____

98. His shiny head made him the butt of occasional jokes on *The Mary Tyler Moore Show* and *Love Boat*.

   _____

99. Once a serious actor, he became a comedy icon thanks to his role as Frank Drebin in the *Police Squad* TV show and *Naked Gun* film series.

   _____

100. This singer joined the ranks of those banned from *Saturday Night Live* after she ripped up a photo of the pope on national television.

   _____

1. **LIBRA**
   Libra is represented by a set of balance scales

2. **A**

3. **SUNDAY**

4. **C**

5. **CROCODILE**
   Though the shirts came to be known as "alligator shirts," the creature depicted is a crocodile.

6. *ANNIE HALL*

7. *ANIMAL HOUSE*

8. *URBAN COWBOY*

9. *THE BLUES BROTHERS*

10. *FLASHDANCE*

11. *SPLASH*

12. **CANCER**

13. **LANCE ARMSTRONG**

14. **"LIVE STRONG"**

15. **KAL-EL**

16. **MOXIE**

17. **BANJO**

18. **PILOT**

19. **APPLE**

20. **D**
    In 1937, Ruth Graves Wakefield substituted semi-sweet chocolate instead of baker's chocolate in a cookie recipe. The resulting treat became popular as Toll House cookies.

21. **LIBERTY**

22. **A "FLASH MOB"**
    The first documented "flash mob" occurred in 2003 in the rug department of Macy's in New York City.

23. **B**

24. **A**

25. **TRUE**
    It's customary in Japan for those blessed with such luck to buy expensive gifts for friends and fellow players. The cost involved in purchasing these gifts is the reason for the insurance.

26. **B**

27. **C**
    Izzy was an amorphous blue blob whose name was short for Whatizit.

28. **D**

29. **JACK RUSSELL TERRIER**
    (a.k.a. PARSON RUSSELL TERRIER)

30. **DALMATIAN**
    The film was a live-action remake of the Disney animated classic *101 Dalmatians*.

31. CHIHUAHUA
Gidget was the Taco Bell
spokescanine.

32. GERMAN SHEPHERD

33. TRUE

34. RORSCHACH TEST
The Rorschach Test is the
psychological exam better known
as the Ink Blot Test.

35. ABO TEST
The ABO test tells your blood type,
which might be A, B, AB, or O.

36. SNELLEN TEST
The Snellen Chart is used as an
eye test; you'd recognize it as the
one with the large E on top.

37. FRIEDMAN TEST
Known as the Rabbit Test, this was
long an accurate and inexpensive
way to test for pregnancy. The
problem was, it killed a lot of rabbits.

38. TURING TEST
The Turing Test measures the
level of artificial intelligence
of computers or other
manufactured devices.

39. *TWELFTH NIGHT*

40. *TURKEY TROT*

41. *THE TWIST*

42. *TAKE THAT*

43. *THE PATRIOT*

44. TRUE

45. TRUE

46. TRUE

47. TRUE

48. FALSE
Eastman invented the word
"Kodak."

49. (BA)CKSTR(EET)

50. (GO)LDTHW(AIT)

51. (JA)CKSTR(AWS)

52. HALF-AND-HALF

53. AND ALL THAT JAZZ

54. "PANAMA"

55. GRAND MARSHAL

56. *PATCH ADAMS*

57. RENEGADE

58. BELGRADE

59. STOCKADE

60. SERENADE

61. MARMALADE

62. DARLING

63. HARVEY ENTERTAINMENT

64. ADOPTION

65. "HERE'S JOHNNY!"

66. *THE HEIDI CHRONICLES*

67. STRAWBERRY SHORTCAKE

68. CABBAGE PATCH KIDS

69. MY LITTLE PONY

70. TICKLE-ME ELMO

71. CARE BEARS

72. TEDDY RUXPIN

73. POUND PUPPIES

74. FURBY

75. ADAM AND THE ANTS

76. B-52's

77. CULTURE CLUB

78. DEVO

79. ELVIS COSTELLO

80. BILLY BOB THORNTON

81. KATHERINE ROSS

82. JUDE LAW

83. LINDSAY LOHAN

84. JOHN WAYNE

85. CHRIS ROCK

86. B
   He was better known by the name Connie Mack.

87. B

88. A

89. 714

90. 360

91. 44

92. 17

93. 108

94. DAN AYKROYD

95. MAYIM BIALIK

96. SHANNEN DOHERTY

97. DEFOREST KELLEY

98. GAVIN MACLEOD

99. LESLIE NIELSEN

100. SINEAD O'CONNOR